Uncover the Secrets of

SAP SALES & DISTRIBUTION

First Edition

Uncover the Secrets of

SAP SALES & DISTRIBUTION

First Edition

Published by

Uncover the Secrets of SAP Sales & Distribution
by Luz Andrea Diaz

Published by Azul Publishing LLC, www.azulpublishing.com,
110 E Houston Street, 7th Floor, San Antonio, TX. 78205

Printed history:
        First Edition: June / 2019

NOTE: Azul Publishing or the author are not associated with SAP AG or its subsidiaries in the US or worldwide.

Feedback Information

At Azul Publishing, our goal is to create in-depth technical books of the highest quality and value.

Each book is created with care and precision, undergoing rigorous development that involves the unique expertise of members from the professional technical community.

Readers' feedback is a natural continuation of this process.

If you have any comments regarding how we could improve the quality of this book, or otherwise alter it to give you a better understanding of the topics covered, you can contact us through email at feedback@AzulPublishing.com.

Please make sure to include the book title and ISBN in your message.

Mrs. Luz Andrea Diaz is a SAP Certified consultant, focusing on making the learning of SAP an easy and streamlined experience.

Luz has over 22 years of experience implementing SAP projects in Latin America, North America and Europe in the following industries: Repetitive Manufacturing, Food and Beverage, Discrete manufacturing, Make to Order Processes, as well as Construction.

Mrs. Diaz holds certifications in SAP Order to Cash, Procure to Pay, Logistics execution (Transportation) processes, ,and it's a certified Project Manager and Scrum Master.

A SAP veteran, she works with customers daily, designing, implement ng and supporting SAP solutions.

In recent years, she has been focusing on the Government sector, and sharing her experience in her online training academy : Consulting Dojo ® (www.ConsultingDojo.com)

Luz lives in Texas with her husband and daughters.

Table of Contents

ACKNOWLEDGMENTS

This book wouldn't have been possible without the support of my family, my beloved husband and my two daughters. All of you are the reason for this book.

I'd also like to thank my editor, Jessica Howard, for the superb work she did polishing the content and helping me look like a rock star author!

Additionally, thanks to my publishing company, Azul Publishing, for giving me the chance to share my experience with people who are starting their SAP career.

And to you, my reader, thank you for letting me be part of your journey to becoming an SAP consultant. On your journey you will encounter roadblocks and detours.

Please think of me as an experienced friend who has traveled the path already and wants to help you make it safe and sound to the promised SAP land!

1.INTRODUCTION

This book is written with the novice reader in mind who is interested in a career in the Systems, Applications, and Products (SAP) consulting world.

It is also intended for a situation, in which SAP is being implemented for the first time, and readers want to understand the terminology and whatever is being discussed or proposed.

And finally, it is intended for a more experienced SAP consultant not familiar with the Sales and Distribution (SD) module. The idea is that, at the end of the book, readers will be able to implement the core functionality of the Order-to-Cash (OTC) process.

Note: As with everything, it is recommended that you practice and play with the system for you to become familiar with it. What we can make sure is that we go into enough detail for you to take it as a base and build upon the concepts learned.

1.1. ORGANIZATION

This book is organized in the order in which we normally perform the configuration and use the master data, as it is required for an implementation project.

Chapters 1 and 2 include an introduction to SAP, where relevant acronyms and basic navigation through the system are discussed. If you are familiar with SAP, or have already read one of our introductory series books (SAP MM Essentials, SAP LE Essentials) and mastered these topics, you can proceed to Chapter 3.

Chapters 3 and 4 detail the building blocks for the system. Chapter 3 will discuss the organizational structure (how your company is represented in the system), and Chapter 4 will discuss the master data required specifically for the SD transactions. If you will not be performing configuration regularly, you will find the "Uses and Functionality" sections, which discuss the process for entering transactions, as well as any relevant information and data required, more useful. However, if you are curious about how the system can be modified to your needs, please refer to the "Configuration" section.

If you are a consultant that is expected to know how to use the functionality and also customize the system for adaptations for your company or project, then you will need to read both the "Uses and Functionality" and the "Configuration" sections.

Chapters 5 through 9 discuss the core functions within SD: sales order, pricing, shipment, and billing documents, as well as printing the relevant documents for those processes. In general, the Order Fulfillment processes go as follows, and as we progress, we will indicate where we are at in the process.

Note: The processes in gray are not covered in this book, as this focuses on the core/basic functionality.

Pricing, discussed in Chapter 5, has its own chapter, given that it is one of the most complicated areas in SD. Once you have mastered the logic and sequences to create your own pricing, other functionalities like output determination, text determination, reconciliation, account determination, etc. will be easier for you to understand, as they all follow the same logic.

Chapter 10 focuses on how to resolve frequent issues, like cancelling an incorrect goods order, processing a return, cancelling invoices, etc.

Chapter 11 shows the standard and useful reports for the SD areas.

Chapter 12 includes a summary of the learned processes.

Chapter 13, the appendix, will include additional information like commonly used transactions in SD and languages supported by SAP.

Be on the lookout for our friend SAPito, who will introduce helpful tips and tricks.

With that being said, let's begin!

2. INTRODUCTION TO SAP

2.1. WHAT IS SAP?

SAP was a company founded in Germany in 1972 by five entrepreneurs who had a vision of creating standard application software for real-time business processing. The idea behind SAP was to interconnect all the company's business areas in a real-time environment and have precise and up to date information so that decisions could be made immediately, if necessary.

Since it's founding, SAP has issued different "releases" (versions), with the most current release being S/4 HANA.

Currently, SAP is used by over 300,000 customers around the world, with many of the Fortune 500 companies running on this platform. At the time this book was written, SAP's plan for future growth is to expand in emerging market economies such as Brazil, India, Russia, and especially China.

It intends to invest some 2 billion euros in the mid-market sector alone.

In the SAP world, you will find countless acronyms and abbreviations, many of which will be discussed in the following chapters.

2.2. ENTERPRISE RESOURCE PLANNING (ERP)

In information technology, enterprise resource planning (ERP) is business process management software that allows an organization to use a system of integrated applications to manage the business and automate many back office functions related to technology, services, and human resources.

ERP software integrates all facets of an operation, including product planning, development, manufacturing, sales and marketing, in a single database, application, and user interface.

There are several different ERP platforms, SAP being one of them.

2.3. CUSTOMER RELATIONSHIP MANAGEMENT (CRM)

In general, **customer relationship management (CRM) includes** all aspects of interactions that a company has with its customers, whether it is sales- or service-related. While the phrase "customer relationship management" is most commonly used to describe a business-to-consumer relationship (B2C), CRM is also used to manage business-to-business (B2B) relationships. Information tracked in a CRM system includes contacts, clients, contract wins, sales leads, and more.

In particular, SAP CRM is a comprehensive solution for managing the company's customer relationships.

It supports all customer-focused business areas, from marketing to sales and service, as well as customer interaction channels, such as the interaction center, the Internet, and mobile clients. SAP CRM is part of SAP Business Suite, and is tightly integrated with SD in R/3.

In many cases, all the CRM orders are downloaded into SAP to complete the fulfillment process, which includes shipping, packing, delivering the goods, and invoicing.

2.4. INTEGRATIONS

In SAP, all modules are somewhat related or integrated with each other In particular, the supply chain modules are tightly integrated to support the OTC (Order to Cash) process.

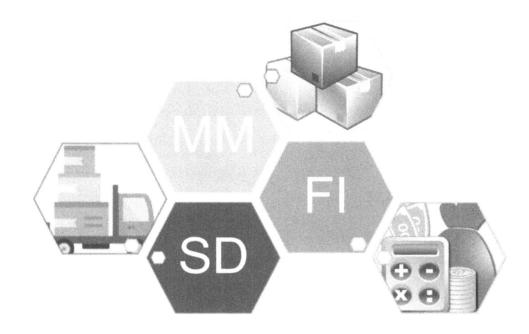

Materials Management (MM) and SD

One of the closest integration with the SD functionality is the Materials Management (MM) module.

In this module, we define the product and services in the material master, so that when a sales quote, an inquiry, or a sales order are placed, we make use of this product code to enter all the items.

Note: Detailed information on this topic is covered in Chapter 4.

Additionally, at sales order capturing time (if defined in the material), an availability check is done for the material, so that we can determine if there will be enough stock to deliver the order on time.

After this, following order entry, the product is picked up from the warehouse, and shipping documents are printed. Upon goods issue, the inventory quantities are reduced automatically.

Financial Accounting (FI) and SD

The module of Financial Accounting (FI) is related to the SD module in the following way: When a sales order is placed, the taxes are determined, with all the rules defined by the finance department. The customer credit limit is also checked according to the maximum amount defined per each customer (if credit check has been defined).

Whenever a goods movement takes place due to a SD document (delivery, returns, etc.), a financial document is created in the background and every one of the movements hits a general ledger (G/L) account. For example, in general, on a goods issue due to a sale, the inventory balance account gets decreased, and the cost of goods sold account balance gets increased.

Note: These are general situations; however, based on company requirements, this financial posting could vary.

Once goods are shipped, an invoice is sent to the customer, which also generates a financial document. Other billing documents (debit memos, credit memos, etc.) also generate financial postings.

Example: In regard to the goods issue, the shipment of goods is reflected in finance.

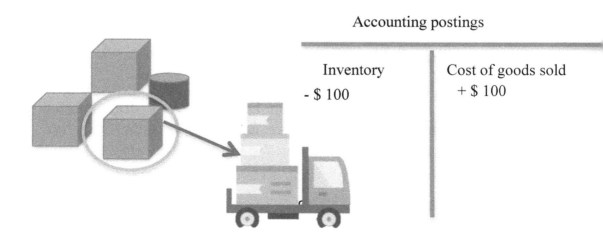

Accounting postings

| Inventory | Cost of goods sold |
| - $ 100 | + $ 100 |

Production Planning (PP) and SD

In regular operations (with Make to Stock [MTS] scenarios), the SD module is integrated with Production Planning (PP) via the transfer of requirements.

In a simplified scenario, this will work as follows:

A sales order for 40 pcs is created.

However, after reviewing current stock levels, the system determines there are only 30 pcs available.

At this time, this requirement is automatically transferred to the PP module with the need to produce 10 more pcs, and based on production time it will confirm the remaining 10 pcs on the sales order for a future time (whenever these pieces will be produced and in stock).

In the production area, whenever the planner runs the Material Requirements Planning (MRP), all these requirements are considered (as well as future demand) to determine the amount of stock to be produced.

In a more complex Make to Order (MTO) scenario, at the moment of the sales order, the list of desired components is included in the document .

This will trigger a planned order that can be directly converted to a production order. In this case, the production order is directly linked to the sales order, and the finished product can only be used by this particular customer.

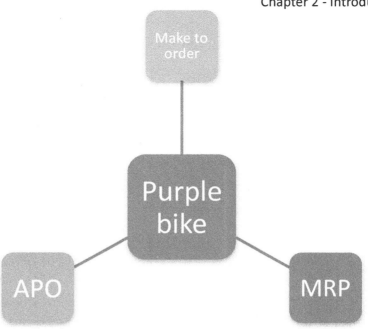

Example: Our Company makes custom bikes according to customer specifications (Make to Order process).

In this case, each sales order will be different, as each one of the bikes will have a different color, trim, height, etc.

3. HOW DO I START?

In SAP, you can usually connect to several environments (servers), which will serve different purposes. A typical system landscape for ERP Central Component (ECC) is as follows:

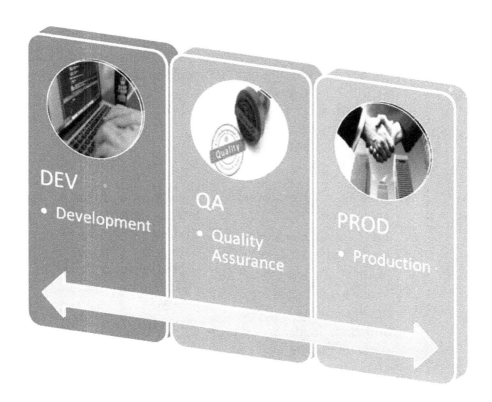

Type	Description	Comments
Development	Normally all ABAP programming for custom developments and reports, as well as customizing, is done here.	**IMPORTANT**: As a standard practice, usually there is a purely development and configuration system where master data and tests are not included. This is known as the "Golden Client". All configuration is copied to the rest of the environments from this environment.
Sandbox	In some cases, a sandbox environment is created to test configuration, developments or data loads without affecting the real configuration.	The environment is open for configuration, master data, etc.
Quality Assurance	This is a pre-production environment. This environment is optional, and not all installations use this server. If used, normally all developments, interfaces, and data loads are tested here before being used in the real production environment.	If this environment is used, after go-live, it is recommended that every certain time, sets of data from the real system are copied into the QA box for tests, validation, and support purposes (if the infrastructure allows it).
Production	This is the online, real-time system used in the company. All company transactions are registered here for the available modules.	Usually all information from this system is backed up. Depending on the data load and database size, an archiving could be done (normally this is done after 5, 10, or 20 years of operations).

A quick comparison between the different environments can help to clarify the differences:

Type	Contains Master Configuration	Open for Configuration Changes *1	Accepts Master Data	Comments
Development (Golden)	Yes	Yes	--	Some minimal master data can be created here if required for configuration. Examples: <ul><li>Financial Accounts</li><li>Vendors</li><li>Customers</li><li>Materials</li></ul>
Sandbox	--	Yes	Yes	
Quality Assurance	--	--	Yes	
Production	--	--	Yes	

*1 – If the environment is not open for configuration, any desired changes to the configuration must be made on the Development client and copied to this system.

3.1. SAP GRAPHICAL USER INTERFACE (GUI)

As with any other application software, you have the option of connecting to SAP via a regular shortcut to the program.

❖ If you have the regular login, you will see an icon on your computer like this:

SAP Logon

❖ To access SAP, double-click on the icon or click **Open** to start the navigation.

For the newer versions of SAP, there are alternate ways to connect (i.e. via a link to a webpage, as shown in the following screen).

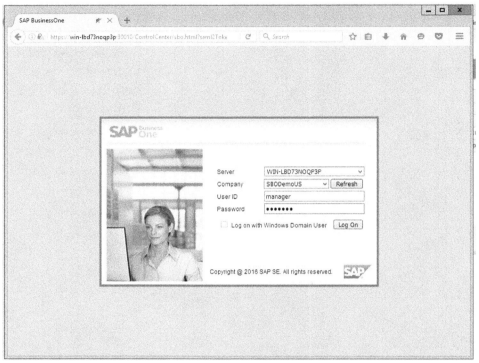

In this book, the screens in the classic GUI installation will be shown, as most customers have not yet migrated to the new online login and transactional screens.

Starting the Navigation

Let's start with the basics of the Graphical User Interface (GUI).

After clicking to open the login window, you will see the systems available to you:

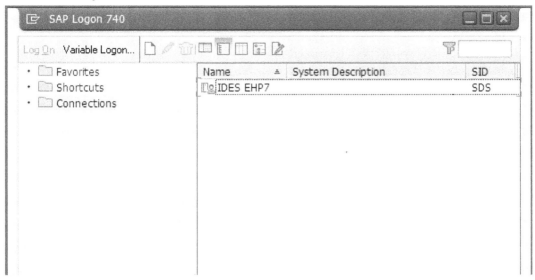

Note: Depending on your system landscape, you will see additional or fewer options.

❖ Once you have selected the system you want to connect to, you can double-click on it, and the initial login screen will appear. If it is your first time to access SAP, you will need to enter:

• Client number
  o This will be the server ID number provided by the administrator
• Your assigned SAP user ID
• Temporary password
• Language
  o Please see the Appendix for SAP's 41 supported languages

❖ Click **Enter** or

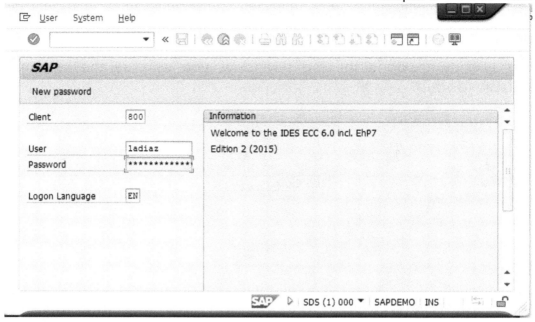

At this time, the system will prompt you to change your temporary password.

Note: You will need to follow your company guidelines for password creation and security.

This step will only be done the first time you access SAP. After that, you will need to enter your newly created password.

Set a password that is easy for you to remember, but not easily identified by another person. If you forget your password, you will have a set number of trials to access it (usually three). If you don't succeed, your username will be locked automatically and you will need to contact your system administrator to unlock it.

3.2. NAVIGATION

To navigate in SAP, you will use the navigation bar at the top of the screen. Here you have the following buttons:

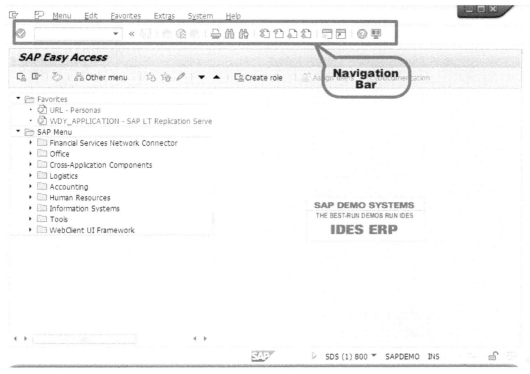

Button	Function	Button	Function
✅	Enter Accept a transaction.		Command Field Enter the code (shortcut) to the desired transaction.

	Save Save any changes or newly recorded information.		Go Back Similar to the internet browser, goes back to the previous transaction. If navigating within a menu, goes back to the previous option in the menu.
	Go Up Navigate to the top menu (if navigating within a menu).		Cancel Cancels the transaction. In case of an error, this button can be used to exit the transaction.
	Print You send a hard copy to the selected printer.		Search Search for a particular value on a report or transaction.
	Search Next Search for the following value found on the report or transaction.		**Page Up** (to top) Navigate to the initial page of a document or report.
	Page Up (one page at a time) Navigate to the previous page on a document or report.		**Page Down** (one page at a time) Navigate to the following page on a document report.

🗗	**Page Down** (last page) Navigate to the last page of the document or report.	▦	New Transaction Window Create a working window, where you can run a separate transaction or report or consult data.
🡕	Create a Shortcut Generate a shortcut of the transaction.	？	Online Help Provides help about the use of a particular field or transaction.
🖳	Customize Local Layout Change parameters like SAP color schema, display key codes on the menus, accessibility options, and set the default directories for local data like "SapWorkDir."		

To navigate to the functionality, you have two options:

Via Menus

If you choose to use the menu option, you will navigate by clicking on a particular folder, and this will open the different options for this menu. Once you reach the desired option, you can double-click on it for the system to show the transaction data.

Example: You want to create a new sales order, so follow the complete path until you reach the desired transaction.

❖ Once there, you double-click on the transaction:

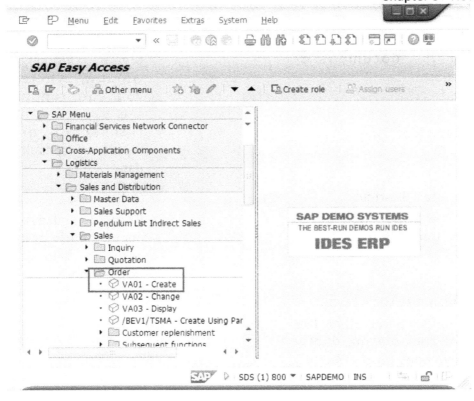

This will take you to the Create Sales Order screen.

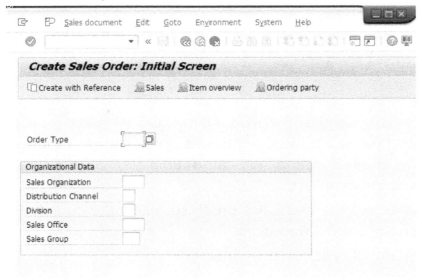

Note: If you want to go back to the previous menu, click the **Back** button.

Via Transaction Code

Once you are more familiar with the system, you can navigate faster via the transaction codes (or t-codes). You can take the scenic route via the menus, or you can use the t-code to create a sales order.

Example: Manually type the t-code for sales order creation (*VA01*) on the command field and click **Enter**.

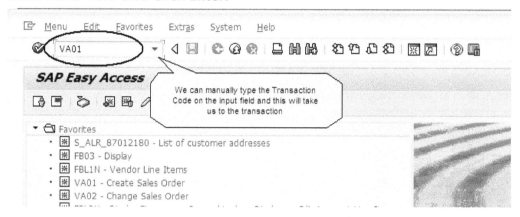

This will take you directly to Create Sales Order screen.

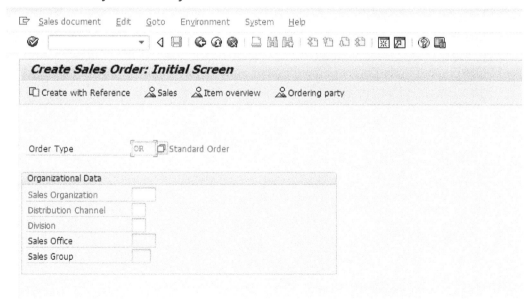

In SAP, most of the operational transactions and functionality have a corresponding t-code.

A list of the most common transactions for SD is provided in the Appendix.

For configuration, not all of the options have a t-code, and you must reach them via the menus.

3.3. CONFIGURATION

In SAP, functionality can be customized according to company requirements, which allows for greater flexibility. The configuration can be accessed via menu or the transaction used for this

The image below shows the menu path for configuration:

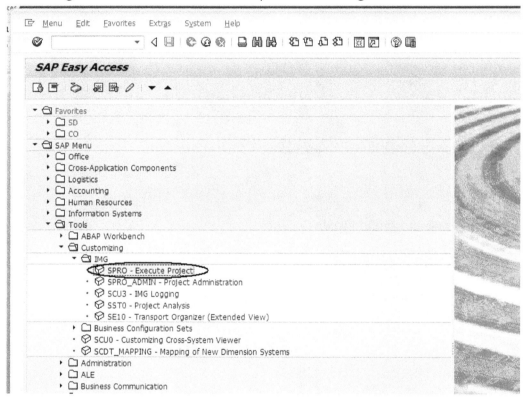

The transaction for customizing is SAP Project Reference Object (SPRO).

You will see your project name and must select it, or, if it is not available, select **SAP Reference IMG**.

You can also use the F5 button.

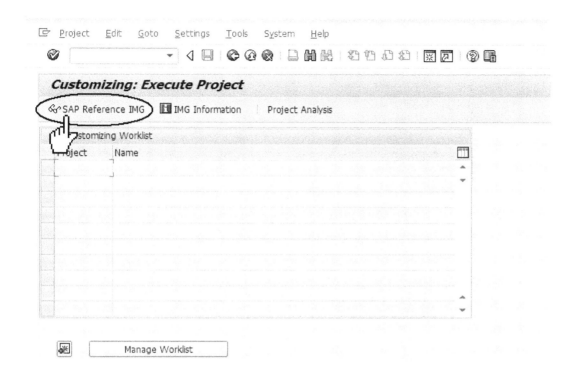

In the following chapters, we will discuss the details of the fundamental concepts of the functionality, and also how to configure it (or adapt it to your organization needs). In addition, we will offer some tips and tricks that will save you headaches later on.

Since this is an introductory book, we will be covering the core functionality for the SD module, marked as follows:

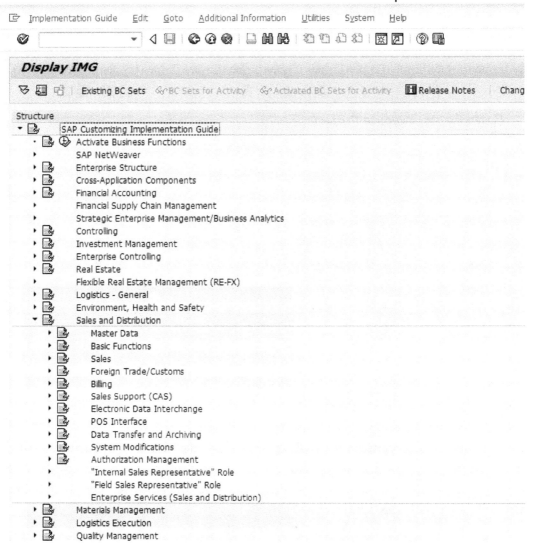

3.4. TRANSPORTS

As mentioned before, there are different environments in the system.

Some of them do not accept direct configuration. To be updated, the configuration must be copied from the development environments.

In SAP, this is done via a "Transport".

A transport is similar to a package, which contains all the changes made to a particular configuration object.

Every time you save a change on the configuration, you will get the option to create a transport or use an existing one.

This will give you a unique identifier (request) number that will be used to copy your configuration from one environment to the other.

If you want to see a list of your transports when creating a new one, click on **Own Requests**.

List of Transports

If you would like to see a detailed list of all the transports you (or any other person) have generated, you will need to access the transaction "Transport organizer."

In this transaction, you can:

- Display a list of all your transports (released, open for changes, etc.)
- View a detailed transport log for the transport (i.e. to which environments it has been copied).
  - o If there was any error while copying the transport, it will be recorded here also.

- Release a transport (discussed in detail in the next section).

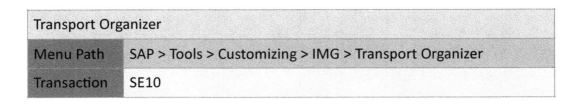

Transport Organizer	
Menu Path	SAP > Tools > Customizing > IMG > Transport Organizer
Transaction	SE10

❖ First, you will need to enter the user ID of the creator of the transport.

Example: User LADIAZ

Note: If you want to see a list of all your available transports mark all the options.

- ❖ Click "ENTER" or select the   button.

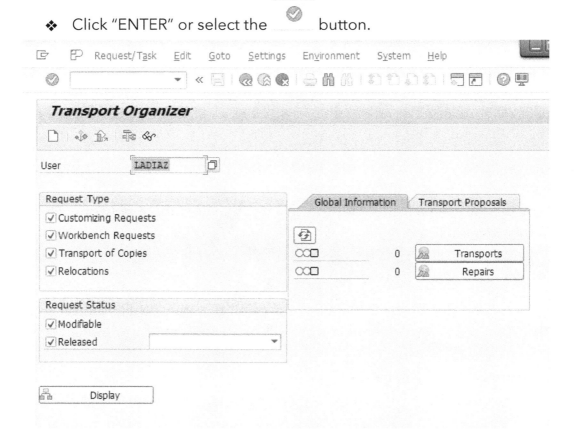

This will bring you a list of all your transports, as shown in the next image.

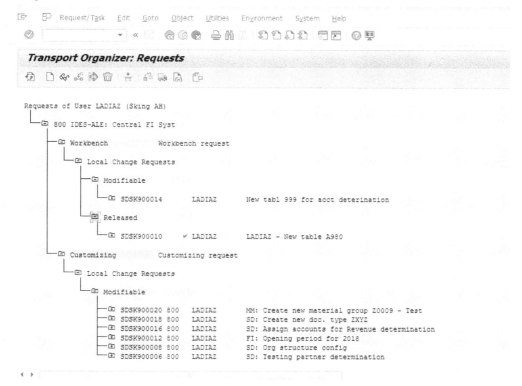

The system will group them by type (Customizing or Workbench) and within those categories as "Modifiable" and "Released."

From this screen, if you need to get the details of the transport or need to update information like description, notes, etc., you can select it and

double-click on the transport number (or use the display option).

By default, the information will appear as display only.

❖ If you need to update it, select the update option, shown on the following screen:

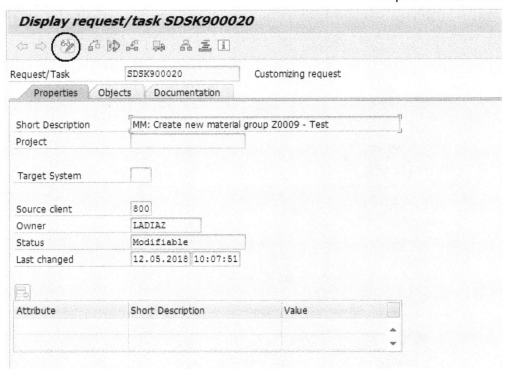

Concept of "Release a Transport"

There are two ways to copy the transport to another environment:

- Manually via a "transport of copies."
- Automatically (for released transports).

In most implementations, the transports are set up to be copied automatically to other environments once they are "released."

Normally, you will only release a transport when tests have been successful, and you are not expecting more changes.

Note: Once a transport has been released, it will not accept any additional changes. If you need to modify the same configuration object, you will need to create a new transport.

Example: You have to configure the name of your company: "Acme Inc."

You configure it and save the changes, generating a "transport".

Unfortunately, you didn't have coffee that morning and ended up configuring: "Acme **Icn.**"

The next day, you realize the error and want to correct it.

What to do?

- If the transport has not been released, you can just make the correction and save it, using the same transport ID number you used originally.
  - This will overwrite the previous incorrect description.
- If the original transport was released, you will have to make the correction and save, but use a new transport ID number.
  - This will overwrite the previous incorrect description.
  - You also need to make sure that both transports are passed in the correct order (first the incorrect one, then the correct one).

Process to Release a Transport

In order to release a transport, you first need to access the transaction "Transport organizer" (the same one mentioned in the previous section to display the transports list.

Transport Organizer	
Menu Path	SPRO > Enterprise Structure > Definition > Financial Accounting > Edit, Copy, Delete, Check Company Code > Edit Company Code Data
Transaction	SE10

❖ Enter the user ID of the creator of the transport.

Example: User LADIAZ

Since we are releasing a transport, mark only the option "Modifiable' and the request type (normally Customizing or Workbench), as shown below:

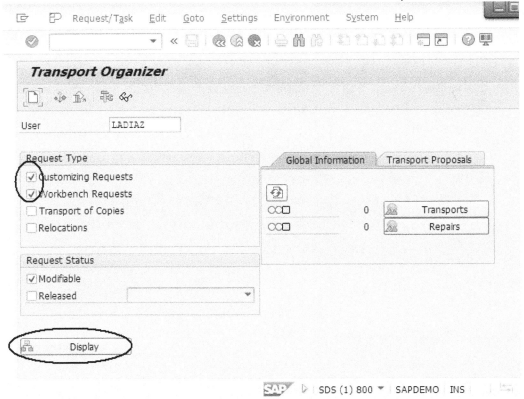

❖ Select **Display** or click "Enter."

After this, you will see the list of available transports for release.

❖ Click on the one you want to release and on the folder to the left of it, click again, so it opens the associated "tasks".

Note: A task is list of the changes you did for a configuration object.

If you used the transport to configure different objects (not recommended), you will have several tasks linked to the main transport.

For the main transport to be available for release, first release each task as follows:

❖ Select the task by clicking on it. After this, select 🚚 to release the transport, as shown in the following image:

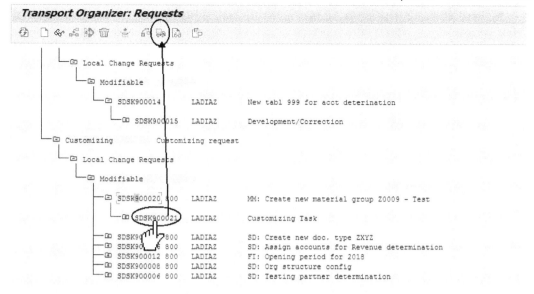

❖ Repeat the process for all the tasks.

Once all the tasks are released, you will be able to release the main transport.

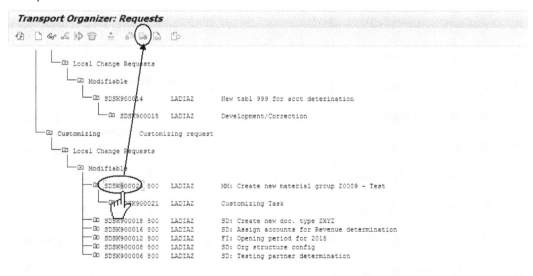

Best Practices

It is a recommended practice to create independent transports for every configuration transaction.

Some people group theirs by day, week, or whichever grouping makes sense to them.

The reason for this is that if your transport fails when being moved between environments and you need to re-generate a new one, if only a few transactions are included, the issue is isolated to it.

On the other hand, if you have all your configurations in only one transport, then you will need to re-do everything.

3.5. EXERCISES

Navigate

- From the initial menu, create a new session
- On the new session, go to the sales order creation transaction (VA01)
- From this session, return to the initial menu

Configuration and Transports

- From the initial menu, go to the configuration
- Open the section to update the plants (see path in section 3.2.2)
- Modify the description of one of the existing plants in your system by adding your initials
- Save the changes, which must generate the transport number
- Go back to the initial screen
- Monitor your transport and make sure it is on the transport lists

4. BUILDING BLOCKS — ENTERPRISE STRUCTURE

The enterprise structure is similar to the foundation of a house.

It needs to be clearly defined before anything else can be build upon it.

In SAP represents how a company is organized legally and logistically.

The correct foundation and creation of an organizational structure is vital, as this will determine the level of information obtained from aggregate reports and standard financial statements.

It has several areas that are determined on a hierarchical level.

Some of the enterprise structure elements are usually defined by the finance areas (like group company or credit control areas), but that is a topic for a finance course.

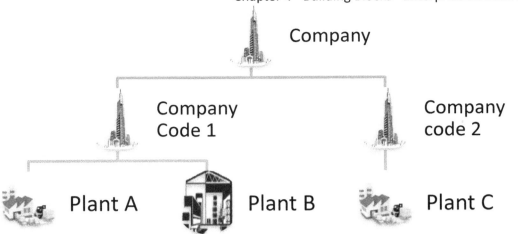

The definition, purpose, and configuration of all the logistics and sales area elements will be discussed in this chapter.

4.1. COMPANY CODE

Uses and Functionality

The company code is the smallest organizational unit of external accounting for which a complete, self-contained set of accounts can be created.

This includes the entry of all transactions that must be posted and the creation of all items for legal individual financial statements, such as the balance sheet and the profit and loss statement.

The definition of the company code organizational unit is **obligatory**.

If you want to manage the accounting for several independent companies simultaneously, you can set up several company codes for one client. You must set up at least one company code for each client.

It is important not to confuse company and company code. Company is normally used for consolidation purposes, and it can be composed of several company codes.

Configuration – Create a New Company Code

Company Code Configuration	
Menu Path	SPRO > Enterprise Structure > Definition > Financial Accounting > Edit, Copy, Delete, Check Company Code > Edit Company Code Data
Transaction	Not available

This section will discuss the procedure to define a new company code from start to finish.

The creation of a company is normally the responsibility of a finance functional consultant. However, it is included in this book, so that in the event that one is not available, you are able to execute this step. Without it, you will not be able to set up the rest of the required sales and distribution functionality.

Use the Copy option to copy any related parameters by default.

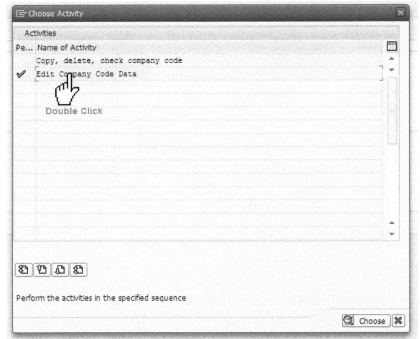

We will use the New Entries option.

❖ Enter the company code ID, as well as the additional data.

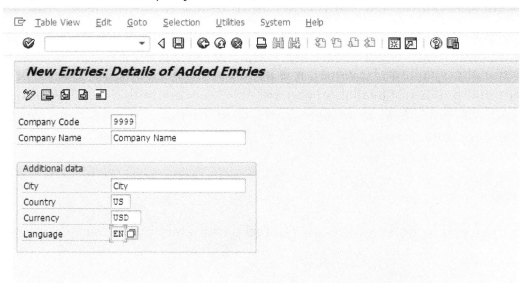

After this, the system will prompt you for the address:

This address information will appear by default on the SAP standard forms for finance-related documents.

❖ After this, you can go back to the initial screen by clicking the **Back** button, where you can then save the newly created company code.

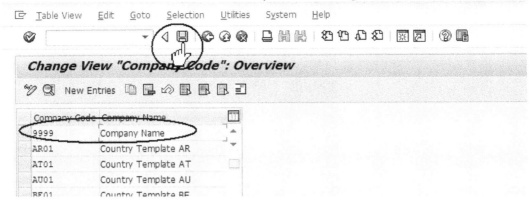

4.2. PLANT

Uses and Functionality

The plant is an operating area or branch within a company.

Normally it represents a production plant, but it can also represent a warehouse, a separate physical area of the company, or even a department.

The plant is embedded in the organizational structure as follows:

•The plant is assigned to a single company code. A company code can have several plants.

•Several storage locations in which material stocks are managed can belong to a plant.

•A plant can have several shipping points. A shipping point can be assigned to several plants.

A plant has the following attributes:

- An address.
- A language.
- Belongs to a country.
- Its own material master data. You can maintain data at plant level for the following views on a material master record in particular: MRP, purchasing, storage, work scheduling, production resources/tools, forecasting, quality management, sales, and costing.

The plant plays an important role in the following areas:

- Material valuation: If the valuation level is the plant, the material stocks are valuated at plant level. If the valuation level is the plant, you can define the material prices for each plant. Each plant can have its own account determination.

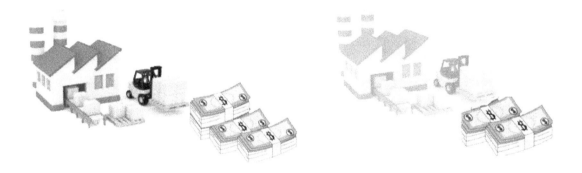

- Inventory management: The material stocks are managed within a plant.
- Production:
  - MRP: Material requirements are planned for each plant. Each plant has its own MRP data. Analyses for materials planning can be made across plants.
  - Costing: In costing, valuation prices are defined only within a plant.

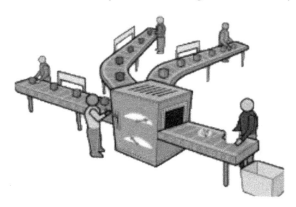

- Plant maintenance: If a plant performs plant maintenance planning tasks, it is defined as a maintenance planning plant. A maintenance planning plant can also carry out planning tasks for other maintenance plants.

Configuration – Creating a New Plant

In this section, we will learn how to create a new plant, copying it with reference to an existing one.

Note: This is a common practice, as copying the existing information brings in from the default plant all the parameters required.

Plant Configuration	
Menu Path	SPRO > Enterprise Structure > Definition > Logistics – General > Define, Copy, Delete Plant
Transaction	Not available

❖ Double-click on Define Plant.

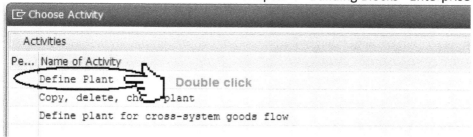

❖ Select default plant 0001 (or any other plant similar to the one you are going to create) and copy it.

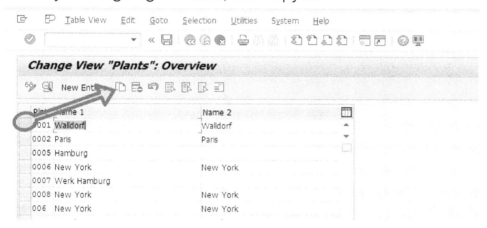

You must enter the new data of the plant, including plant ID, name 1, name 2, country code, city code, and the factory calendar.

IMPORTANT: The factory calendar determines the "working days" for the plant/warehouse/shipping location, etc.

Each plant can have a different factory calendar.

This is important because the "working days" are taken into consideration for calculating the estimated delivery date for the goods.

Change View "Plants": Details

✎ New Entries   ▯ ▯ ▱ ▱ ▱ ▱ ▱

Plant	9999
Name 1	NEW PLANT
Name 2	NEW plant

Detailed information

Language Key	
House number/street	
PO Box	
Postal Code	
City	
Country Key	
Region	
County code	
City code	0001 City code in
Tax Jurisdiction	
Factory calendar	US USA

After clicking **Enter**, the system will prompt you for the address of the plant.

  ❖ Enter in all the known address data.

This address information will appear by default on the SAP standard forms for logistics-related documents (like bill of lading, delivery, shipment documents, etc.)

❖ After this, go back to the initial screen, where you can save the newly created plant.

Configuration – Assign the Plant to a Company Code

Plant Configuration	
Menu Path	SPRO > Enterprise Structure > Assignment > Logistics – General > Assign Plant to Company Code
Transaction	OX18

Once the plant is created, it must be assigned to a company code. This will indicate financially the relationship between the plant and the company, creating the hierarchical structure.

A plant can belong exclusively to only one company code.

One company code can have associated many plants to it.

In this case, you will start with a new assignment to the company code.

❖   Select New Entries.

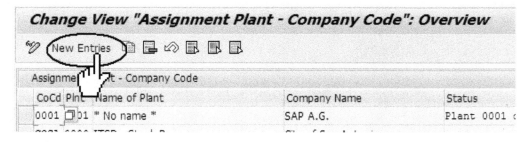

❖   Enter the company code ID and plant ID and click **Enter**. This will return you to the original screen, where you can save the changes.

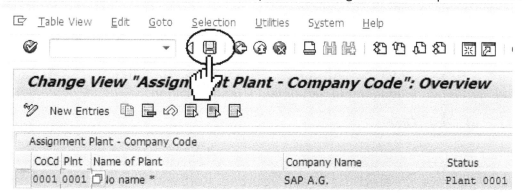

4.3. STORAGE LOCATION

Uses and Functionality

The storage location represents where the inventory is stored physically.

It can also represent different storage types (climate controlled, refrigerated, warehouse, etc.).

In sales and distribution, all materials are issued from a particular plant and storage location.

Although not commonly used, if required, the combination of different factors like shipping conditions, loading group of the material and plant, plus the use of a particular storage location can determine a separate shipping point.

If integration with the warehouse module is active, each storage location can be configured with its own set of WM rules.

Configuration – Creating a New Storage Location

Plant Configuration	
Menu Path	SPRO > Enterprise Structure > Definition > Materials management > Maintain storage location
Transaction	OX09

Once you have created the plant, you can start with the creation of the storage locations.

❖ First, follow the path or the corresponding transaction.

❖ Once there, enter the Plant ID where you will create the new storage location. All the storage locations created at this point will belong to the same plant.

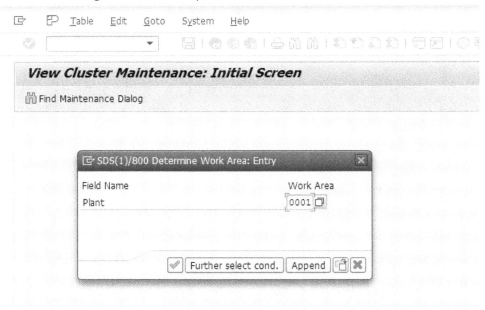

❖ Press Enter or the ✓ button.

Then you will see the storage locations already created for the plant.

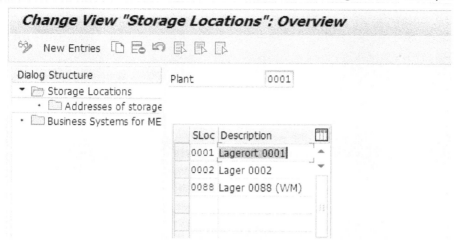

❖ To add a new storage location, select **New Entries** and enter:

• ID – Alphanumeric – 4 characters

• Description – Alphanumeric – 16 characters

Example: Creating a new storage location: "FG01 – Finished Goods1".

The standard and SAP recommended practice is to use numeric assignments for the Storage locations ID, with a reference to the plant number, if possible.

If you have several plants, it is also recommended to maintain consistency in the naming conventions for the storage locations.

Example:

Plant	Storage Locations
1000	1001 – Raw materials 1002 - Semi finished 1003 – Finished goods 1004 – Spare parts
2000	2001 – Raw materials 2002 - Semi finished 2003 – Finished goods 2004 – Spare parts

4.4.   SALES ORGANIZATION

Uses and Functionality

This is one of the most important elements in the SD module, as it is part of the sales area that is needed in all SD documents.

The sales organization normally represents the sales structure for the sales force within a company. It can be geographical, by company, by product lines, etc.

Legally, a sales organization is included in exactly one company code.

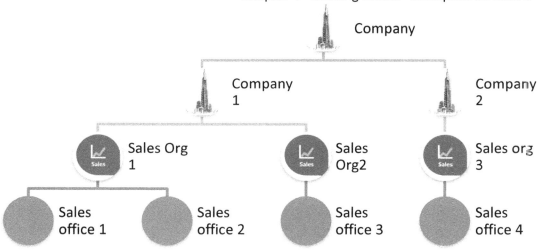

You can assign one or more plants to one sales organization.

Each sales organization has an address.

Within a sales organization, you can define your own master data.

This allows a sales organization to have its own customer and material master data, as well as its own conditions and pricing. You can also define your own sales document types within a sales organization, in addition to assigning sales offices and your own employees to a sales organization.

All items in sales and distribution documents, delivery documents, or billing documents belong to a sales organization.

A sales organization is the highest summation level (after the organizational unit client) for sales statistics with its own statistics currency.

The summation in reports is done at sales organization level.

Example: The Company will like to see how much has been sold annually by region; therefore, sales organization at a regional level is defined.

The sales organization is used as a selection criterion for the lists of sales documents and for the delivery and billing due list. For each sales organization, you can determine the printer for output differently based on sales and billing documents.

A sales organization cannot share any master data with other sales organizations. The master data must be created separately. The data for a distribution channel or a division can, however, is created for several distribution channels or divisions.

Configuration – Creating the Sales Organization

Plan T Configuration	
Menu Path	SPRO > Enterprise Structure > Definition > Sales and Distribution > Define, Copy, Delete Sales Organization
Transaction	OVX5

As mentioned before, the sales organization is one of the most important elements of configuration in the enterprise structure for Sales and Distribution.

In this section, we are going to copy the standard sales organization "0001", as it has most of the required parameters. Be aware that the standard sales organization is defined for Germany, so please be sure to adjust the relevant currency and sales organization for your particular country.

❖ First, select the **Define Sales Organization** option.

❖ Select the sales organization you will take as reference and select copy.

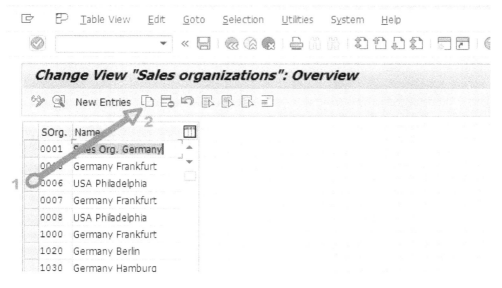

❖ Enter the relevant information for your sales organization.

Table View   Edit   Goto   Selection   Utilities   System   Help

Change View "Sales organizations": Details of Selected Set

Sales Organization   9999 My Sales Organizatio

Detailed information

Statistics currency	USD		
Address text name	ADRS_SENDER	RefSorg.SalesDocType	
Letter header text	ADRS_HEADER	Cust.inter-co.bill.	
Footer lines text	ADRS_FOOTER	Sales org.calendar	US
Greeting text name	ADRS_SIGNATURE		
Text SDS sender		☐ Rebate proc.active	

ALE : Data for purchase order

Purch. Organization		Plant	
Purchasing Group		Storage Location	
Vendor		Movement Type	
Order Type			

Important fields:

Field	Use
Statistics Currency	The currency is used on the reports generated for this sales organization. This currency will also be used as the default currency for documents created for this particular sales org (but users can change it whenever they want to).
A d d r e s s T e x t N a m e / L e tt e r Header Text/Footer Lines Text/Greeting Text Name/Text SDS Sender	The values mentioned in these boxes are standard texts which we maintain using transaction SE78. **Note**: Please see appendix on how to maintain these texts. This could be used as the default address header/footer texts in smart forms/sap scripts for this sales org. **Example:** Invoices, Bill of Lading, Shipment documents.
RefSorg.SalesDocTy pe	This is a reference to another sales organization. The documents we had defined for that other reference organization will be used for our sales org. **Example:** If we are defining sales org 0001 and we put 0002 then sales org 0001 will use document types defined for sales 0rg 0002 only. ⓞ⊙ This can save you work if you have 10 sales orgs. Since all of them will use the same set of documents, then you create your first sales org, and the rest will make reference to the first one (avoiding to define the set of documents to use for the other 9).
Cust. Interco Bill	Mention the customer number here that would be used as the customer for this sales org for intercompany billing. **Note**: The customer number could be different between your different environments (DEV, QA, PRO). This is a customer you create on the customer master.
Sales Org. Calendar	Calendar that would be used for this sales org. **Note**: This calendar can be used to determine dates available for shipping. **Example**: Let's assume that Jan 01 is deemed as non-working day. Then shipping date will be Jan 02 (even though product is available on Jan 01).

Rebate Proc. Active	Check this check box if you want to have rebate processing for this sales org.
ALE Data for purchase order	Details mentioned under this block would be used as default values if you are creating purchase order using ALEs/IDOCs (Inbound) only for this sales org.

❖ After this, enter address details for the sales organization.

IMPORTANT: The address for the sales organization is used in the printed forms, as a default from the origin of the products.

Configuration – Assigning the Sales Organization to the Company Code

Assigning the Sales Organization to the Company Code	
Menu Path	SPRO > Enterprise Structure > Assignment > Sales and Distribution > Assign Sales and Distribution to Company Code
Transaction	Not available

Once you have created the company code and the sales organization, you can make the assignments between them.

❖ Assign the sales organization to the company code and save.

As mentioned before, a sales organization can belong only to one company code.

On the other hand, a company code can have several sales organizations associated to it.

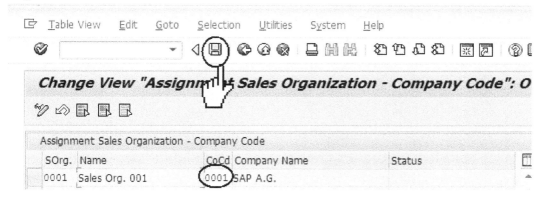

4.5. DISTRIBUTION CHANNEL

Uses and Functionality

A distribution channel is mainly defined to take care of different types of sales in a sales organization. You can define a distribution channel for direct sales, Internet sales, sales through dealers, etc.

This is mainly how the company reaches its consumers (retail, direct, internet, wholesale, etc.)

The most important points for distribution channel are:

- You allocate a distribution channel to one or more sales organizations.
- You allocate one or more plants to a distribution channel.
- Within a distribution channel, you can define your own master data for customers or materials, as well as your own conditions and pricing.
- You can create master data for a representative distribution channel, which is then also used in other distribution channels. To do this, you have to additionally create the allocation of the representative distribution channel to the other distribution channels.
- For a distribution channel, you can determine your own sales document types.
- You can determine sales offices for a distribution channel.

- All items of a sales document belong to a distribution channel. The entire sales document is therefore entered for a distribution channel.

- The items of a delivery can belong to different distribution channels.

- All items of a billing document belong to a distribution channel.

- The distribution channel can be used as a selection criterion in lists.

- You can determine the printer destination for messages differently for every distribution channel on the basis of the sales and billing documents.

Configuration – Creating the Distribution Channel

Create a Distribution Channel	
Menu Path	SPRO > Enterprise Structure > Definition > Sales and Distribution > Define, Copy and Delete Distribution Channel
Transaction	OVXI

This section will focus on configuring a new distribution channel.

❖ For this process, start by selecting **Define distribution channel**. To speed up the process, copy the configuration from an existing distribution channel.

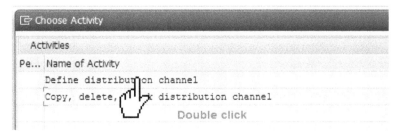

❖ Click the copy icon.

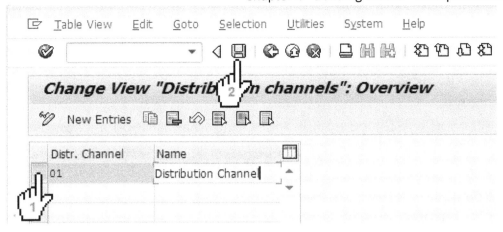

❖ Enter your new ID, a description for the distribution channel, and click the save icon.

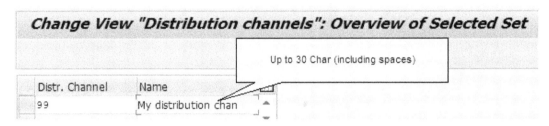

Configuration – Assign the Distribution Channel to a Sales Org

Assign a Distribution Channel to a Sales Org	
Menu Path	SPRO > Enterprise Structure > Assignment > Sales and Distribution > Assign Sales and Distribution Channel to Sales Org
Transaction	Not available

Once the sales organization and the distribution channels are created independently, the next step is to link them by "assigning" the distribution channel for the sales organization.

IMPORTANT: The same distribution channel can be associated to several sales organizations.

Example: The sales organization 1000 and 2000 can be associated to the same distribution channels: "Retail" and "Online".

Additionally, sales organization 1000 can also have the "Wholesale" distribution channel.

❖ To start with the assignment of the distribution channel, select an appropriate distribution channel and sales organization and click the copy icon to create a new combination.

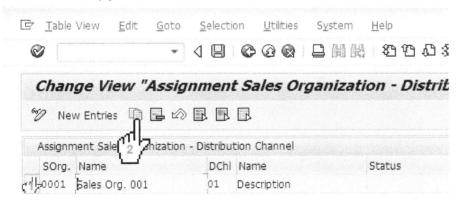

❖ Enter the sales organization and distribution channel.

SOrg.	Name	DChl	Name	Status
0001	Sales Org. 001	01	⬚scription	

Assignment Sales Organization - Distribution Channel

Note: If you have several distribution channels, you will need to create new entries to be able to assign all of them to your sales organization.

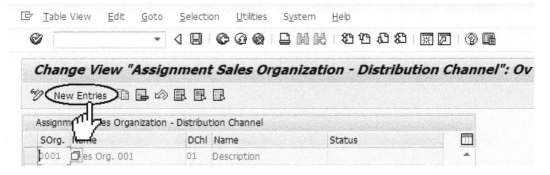

If you have a large amount of combinations for sales org and distribution channels, you can create an Excel file with the required data and copy and paste your values in the corresponding columns here.

Note: Do this for only whatever rows are available on your screen, as SAP will not scroll down for additional values.

4.6. DIVISION

Uses and Functionality

A division in SAP represents a product group or product line. It can also represent something totally different, like a department.

In the following graph, Acme Inc. has structured the divisions by types of products:

- Tablets
- Printers

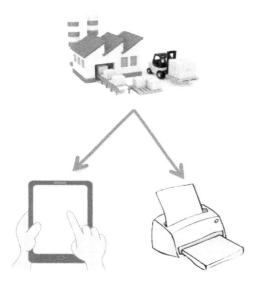

Typically, the material master record will belong to a particular division. Examples:

- The tablets will be assigned to the division "01 – Tablets"
- The printers will be assigned to the division "02 – Printers"

In other cases, you can create a "general" division that will be assigned to the material, as any division can sell it.

General materials will be assigned to division "03 – General tech".

Examples: In Acme Inc., during Christmas time, both divisions sell "USB drives".

- The material "USB Drive" will be assigned to division "03 – General tech".

Another company ("Consulting Dojo Inc.") sells training services, so the different divisions will represent the main areas the company has:
- 001 – Training
- 002 - Books
- 003 – Consulting
- 004 – Conferences
-

Configuration – Creating a Division

Creating a Division	
Menu Path	SPRO > Enterprise Structure > Definition > Logistics – General > Define, Copy, Check Division
Transaction	Not available

This section will focus on creating divisions.

For this configuration, we will start from scratch, not copying the information from a reference, for you to see the difference in the procedure.

The division creation is a very simple process. We need to define only two fields:
- Division ID
- Name

SAP provides the standard division "01" which can be used as a reference.

Let's start with the process:
- ❖ Select the **Define Division** option.

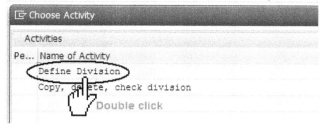

❖ Select New Entries.

Note: In this case we will not copy, as the results are the same as creating a new entry.

❖ Enter your new division ID and name and click the save icon.

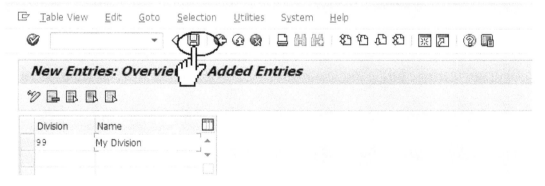

Configuration – Assign the Division to a Sales Organization

Creating a Division	
Menu Path	SPRO > Enterprise Structure > Assignment > Sales and Distribution > Assign Sales Organization – Division
Transaction	Not Available

Once the division and the sales organizations are created, you can add the possible combinations to the sales organizations (similar to what was done for the distribution channels).

The same division can be assigned to different sales organizations.

A sales organization can have also several divisions.

You can also define "reference" divisions, as if you could have tens or hundreds of possible combinations (depending on the size of your organization).

Let's start with the assignment of the division to the sales organization.

In this case, you need to add a new line for each sales organization - division combinations.

❖ Assign the division to your sales organization by selecting **New Entries**.

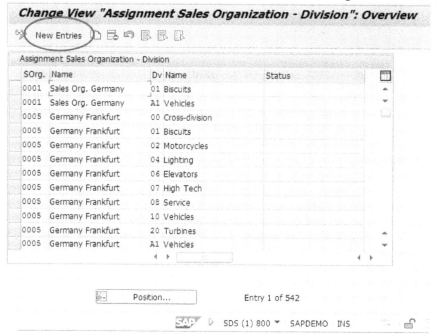

Note: If you had used the copy function previously, your division might already be assigned to a sales organization. If this is combination is not valid, delete this assignment.

❖ Enter all the allowed combinations for your sales organizations and divisions and click the save icon.

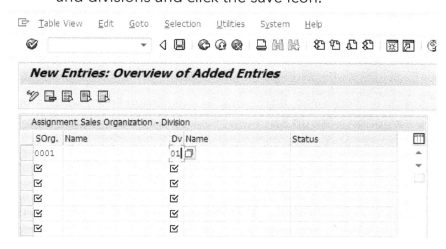

Note: One sales organization can be assigned to several divisions. For every combination, you need to enter one line.

4.7. SALES AREA

Uses and Functionality

SD is organized according to sales organization, distribution channel, and division. A combination of these three organizational units forms the sales area. Creating a sales area allows you to exclude certain combinations of the different organizational areas.

This element is mandatory in most of the sales transactions, so it needs to be defined prior to move on to other processes.

The following drawing illustrates how a sales area can be interpreted.

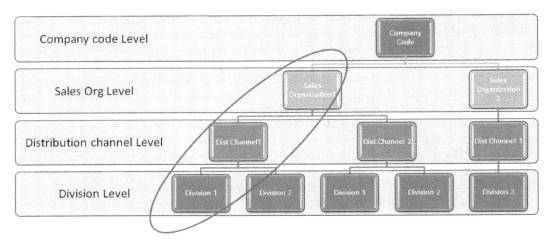

Configuration – Defining the Sales Area

Defining the Sales Area	
Menu Path	SPRO > Enterprise Structure > Assignment > Sales and Distribution > Set up Sales Area
Transaction	Not Available

This section will focus on creating a new sales area (which is the combination of the sales organization, distribution channel, and division).

❖ Start by selecting **New Entries**.

❖ Then, enter the combinations for the allowed sales organizations, distribution channel, and divisions, and click the save icon.

IMPORTANT: In this option, include all the possible combinations you might have for the different elements, as if the combination is not defined, you will NOT be able to create master data and documents for it.

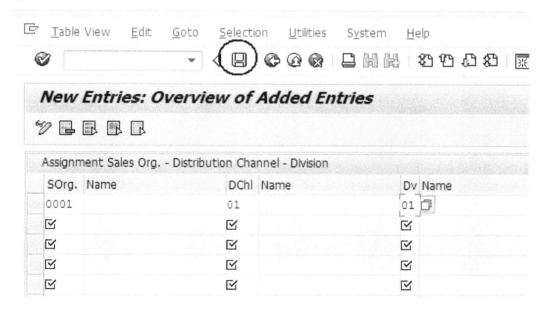

If you have a large number of sales organizations, distribution channels, and divisions, you can prepare an Excel file with all your possible combinations (including the three columns, in the order they appear on the configuration) and copy the information from the worksheet to SAP.

Note: You can't copy all of them at once. The number of rows you have available will depend on your screen resolution and your monitor.

Example. Let's assume you have the following Organizational Structure:

- Sales organizations: 0001, 0002
- Distribution channel: 01, 02
- Division: 01 – 07.

Then you will have 28 possible combinations. The Excel file will look something like this:

6	0001	01	06
7	0001	01	07
8	0001	02	01
9	0001	02	02
10	0001	02	03
11	0001	02	04
12	0001	02	05
13	0001	02	06
14	0001	02	07
15	0002	01	01
16	0002	01	02
17	0002	01	03
18	0002	01	04
19	0002	01	05

4.8.   EXERCISES

- Create a new company code for your country (You can use company 0001 as a reference).

Hint: Remember to change the country in your new company. Company code number: _____

- Create a new plant for your country (You can use Plant 0001 as a reference).

Hint: Remember to change the parameters related to country. Plant number _____

- Create a new sales organization for your company. Sales org # _____

- Create a new distribution channel for your company. Distribution channel # _____

- Create a new division for your company. Division # _____

- Assign your new plant to your new company code. _____

- Assign your new sales organization to your new company code. _____

- Assign your new distribution channel to your sales organization. _____

- Assign your new division to your sales organization. _____

- Create a new sales area with your new organizational structures created. New sales area _____

5. MASTER DATA

In general, the master data is a company's directory for customers, vendors, and employees. It also includes the list of all the materials and services the company uses in its operations, in addition to the price lists for the materials.

In keeping with our example from the previous chapter, if the organizational structure is the building blocks of a company, the master data is the furniture and machinery, necessary to complete the day-to-day operations of the organization.

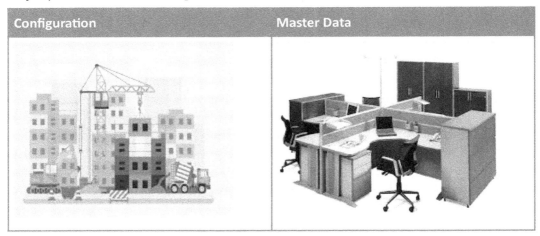

Configuration	Master Data

There are additional elements like "Customer – Material Information Records" that are combinations of information between the lists mentioned above.

5.1. BUSINESS PARTNERS (CUSTOMERS, VENDORS, EMPLOYEES, ETC.)

Uses and Functionality

A business partner role is used to classify a business partner in business terms. The roles assigned to a business partner reflect the functions the partner has and the business transactions in which it is likely to be involved. A business partner role is used for classification purposes during data exchange with SAP ERP.

The usual partners used on sales in distribution are:
- Sold-to *AG* - Who goods are sold to
- Ship-to *WE* - Who goods are shipped to *has a particular address*
- Bill-to *RE* - Who invoice is sent to
- Payer *RG* -- Who invoice is paid by

Example: Imagine we are a big retail chain (Wal-mint), with stores all over the country, and we sell SAP books to them.

In our customer master, we could see something like this:
- 10000001 – Sold-to - Wal-mint Inc.
- 50000001 – Ship-to - Wal-mint Chicago, IL
- 50000001 – Ship-to - Wal-mint Los Angeles, CA
- 30000001 – Bill-to - Wal-mint Headquarters
- 40000001 – Payer - Wal-mint Financial Services

Note: The number ranges mentioned here are fictitious. A customer account group can define a different number range.

In this case, we will not see how to configure a new account group, but we will show you how to create a new customer, since it will be required for the exercises, as well as for your company or project. Also, we will see the most important fields in the customer master relevant for SD operations.

Functionality – Creating a New Customer

Creating a New Customer	
Menu Path	SAP Menu > Logistics > Sales and distribution > Master Data > Business Partner > Customer > Create > Complete
Transaction	XD01

Note: If you are interested only in creating the customer for SD, you can use transaction "VD01 – Create Customer for Sales and Distribution".

❖ Enter the account group.

Note: The account group will determine number ranges and screen layouts (mandatory/optional/hidden fields), as well as partner functions available for the customer.

The account group is used as way to group general types of customers.

The most common account groups used are:

- Customer (General) - Used for General customers.
- Branch – Used for intercompany sales.
- One Time Customers – Used for customers who normally wouldn't be registered as a customer (either because the amount of sales is minimal or because we are selling them a product/ service not normally sold by the organization).

If you want to use an existing customer as a reference, you can fill out the "reference fields".

As a result, most of the information from the original customer will be copied to the new one, making the master data creation easier and faster.

Note: The reference data will only be captured if you are copying an existing customer to a new customer.

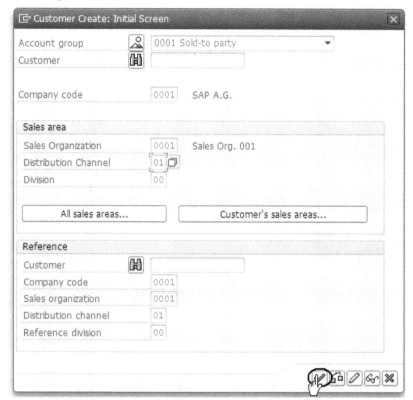

❖ Click the enter icon.

The customer master is grouped into several tabs, called "views". There are normally between 13-15 active views for customers (or more, depending on if you are using a particular industry solution which requires specific information).

The minimum views that are normally needed for every client are:

- General
    - Address
    - Control Data
    - Payment Transactions
- Company Code data
    - Account management
- Sales Area Data
    - Sales

- ○ Billing
- ○ Partner functions

5.1.1.1.General View

As its name suggests, the general view contains general information for the customer.

This information is common to all Sales Areas extended to the customer, so if it's changed here, it changes for all the sales areas.

In the first tab, "Address", contains the customer name, telephone, fax, email, etc.

❖ Enter the general data (name, address, telephone) for the customer and navigate to the Sales Area Data tab.

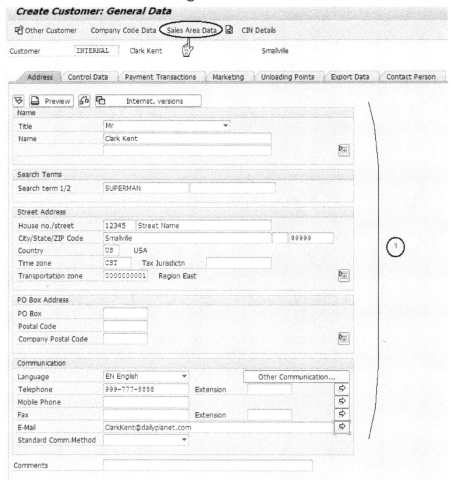

5.1.1.2. Sales Views - Sales

This view contains the corresponding information for SD-related sales operations.

Much of the information entered here will be used as a default on the sales order, so the more information entered here at the time of customer creation (or update), the less information will be required at the time of the sales order.

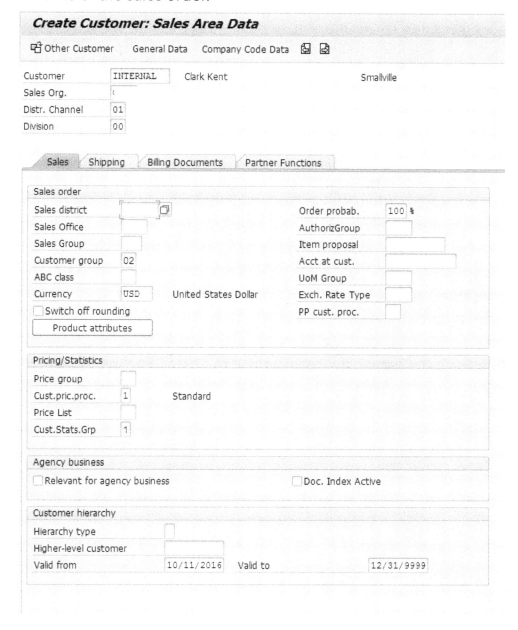

Field	Use
Sales District/ Office/Group	Can be used for pricing, output determination (printouts), and other validations. Will be used as default information for the sales orders.
Customer Group	Grouping of customers. Can be customized for your organization. **Example**: Government, auto Industry, retail, individual sales.
ABC Class	Classification of "importance" for a customer. **Note**: All customers are important, but we could have for example: A – VIP customers, B – Silver status customers, C – Bronze status customers.
Currency	The default currency for the customer.
Price Group	A general grouping that will allow creation of specific pricing and promotions (or surcharges) to a group of customers. Can be in addition to the customer group. Example: 01 – Frequent buyer 02 – Occasional buyer
CustPricingProc	Will help to determine the pricing procedure.
CustStatsGrp	Customer Statistics Group. In order to get information on the sales information system, it is required that this field be active, as well as the same field on the material master.

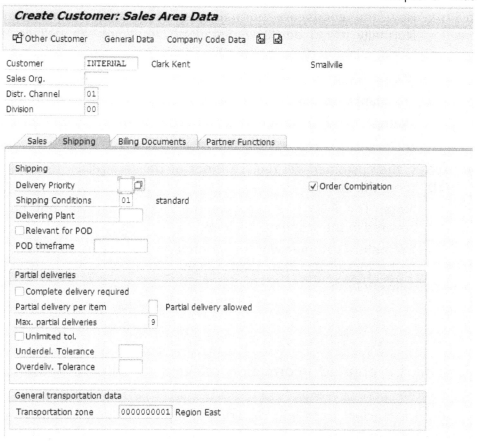

Field	Use
O r d e r Combination	Allows the combination of several sales orders on the same shipments.
	Note: This is normally done to optimize delivery costs although there are some customers that for logistical/procedural reasons will require the independent shipment of their orders.
D e l i v e r y Priority	Can be used to prioritize deliveries in the warehouse and also be used for pricing.
	Example: Customer always requires priority orders, so it is charged an additional premium for every order (based on this field).
	When processing the shipments, this will show as high priority and the warehouse personnel can pick/pack/ship the goods prior to other customer orders.

Shipping Conditions	How the goods are normally delivered to the customer. Normally it will be "01 – Standard" (meaning we deliver). Other customers may use "02 – Pick up" where goods are picked up at the plant/offices.
Delivering Plant	The plant that will ship the goods for this customer by default. **Example**: The customer wants all goods to be shipped from a specific plant because it is close to their plant.
Relevant for POD / POD timeframe	If the customer will require Proof of Delivery (POD) to send them the invoice. **Note**: The POD is a separate transaction that will not be covered in the scope of this book. **Example**: Customer wants a printed goods receipt document to be picked up from their system, stamped and signed at delivery time.

5.1.1.3. Sales Views – Billing View

In this view will be entered information relevant to sales orders and billing documents.

The information included here will be copied for the billing document and invoices.

This tab will also contain all the taxation information.

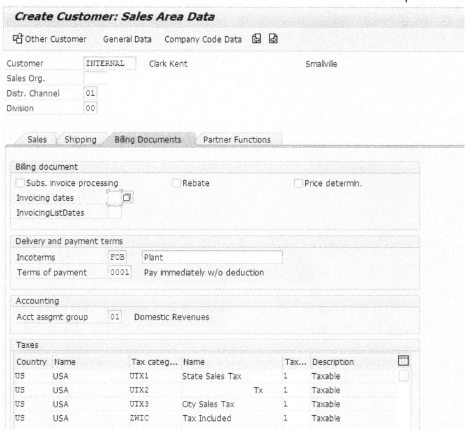

Field	Use
Incoterms	Normally used for documenting the terms of shipping agreed between the two companies (selling, buying). These are internationally recognized terms. **Example**: DAF (Delivered at Frontier) – (City) = We will deliver the goods only up to the border, and the customer will be in charge of picking goods and crossing the border, plus arranging any customs duty declarations.
Terms o f Payment	How the customer will be paying for the goods/services after the invoice has been sent. **Note**: Normally the dates for payment start counting from invoice date.

Account Assignment Group	Customer classification that will help to determine the appropriate revenue account. Normally: 01 – Domestic (within country) 02 – Exports 03 – Affiliate companies **Note**: It can be customized to have additional values, and via this customization, the different revenue accounts can be determined.
Tax	Indicates if the customer is susceptible to pay taxes. In the sales order pricing, the tax procedure will take the customer and the material into consideration to determine if taxes are appropriate or not. **Example**: For non-profit customer (like schools, churches, etc.), it has been deemed that they will not pay taxes for the year, even though they buy materials that are normally taxed. Normally: 0 – Do not pays taxes 1 – Pays full taxes – Other tax percentage

5.1.1.4. Sales Views – Partner Functions

This view displays all customer numbers associated with this customer. All numbers are internal, and once the data is saved, the customer number will be updated.

Please note that upon creation of the sold-to party, all the partner functions appear with the same number. However, it can be associated to different customer numbers, according to organization needs.

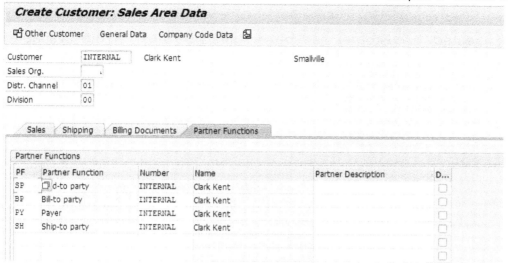

Once the customer is saved, the automatic number will appear, and all the partner functions will be updated automatically.

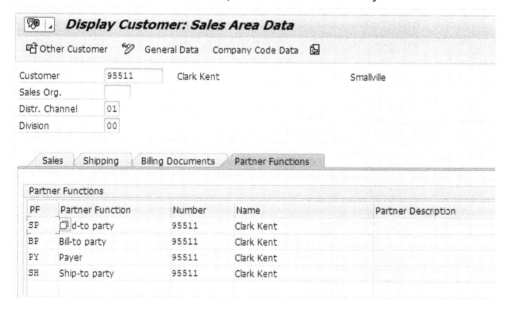

Functionality – Modifying an Existing Customer

Once created, a customer can be modified in most of the available fields.

Note: Once you have orders, invoices and transactional data, some fields are not updatable anymore.

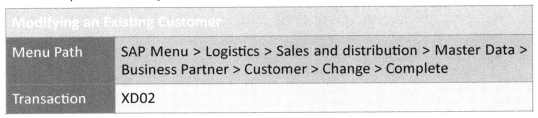

Modifying an Existing Customer	
Menu Path	SAP Menu > Logistics > Sales and distribution > Master Data > Business Partner > Customer > Change > Complete
Transaction	XD02

To update the customer, you need to enter the customer ID and the organizational data.

Since the customer could have been replicated to several company codes and sales areas, make sure you select the appropriate one.

If you leave the information about company code or sales area empty, the only information you will be able to modify will be contained under the General tab.

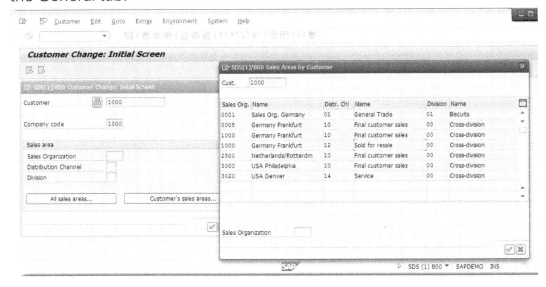

The following image shows the difference in the available screens with and without organizational data:

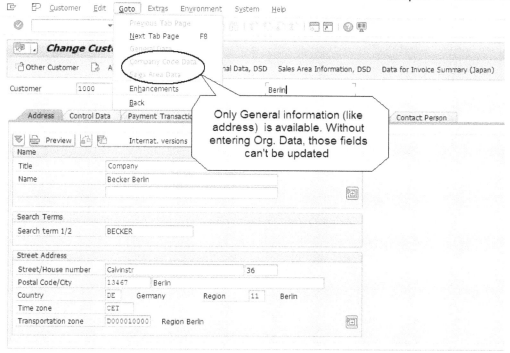

The image below shows how to update an existing customer with organizational data:

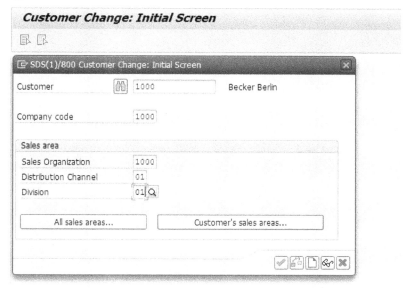

The image below displays all the information for the company code and sales organization entered:

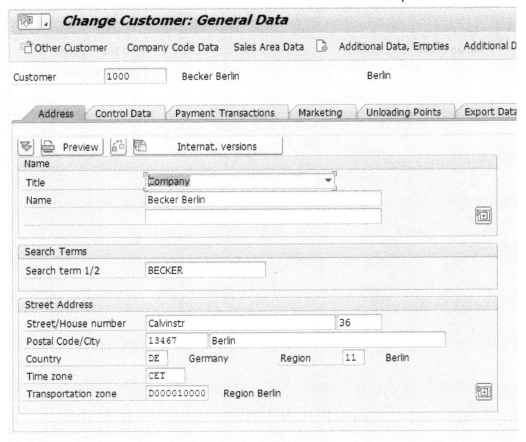

IMPORTANT: For every customer, the information regarding the company code and sales areas can vary, with the exception of general data like name, address, payment transactions, etc.

If the customer is "extended" into several sales areas, and a change must be done to a particular field across all sales areas, the same change must be done manually to each of them.

This is important because these differences in master data can create inconsi

stencies on the operations.

❖ Once the desired information has been updated, save the changes.

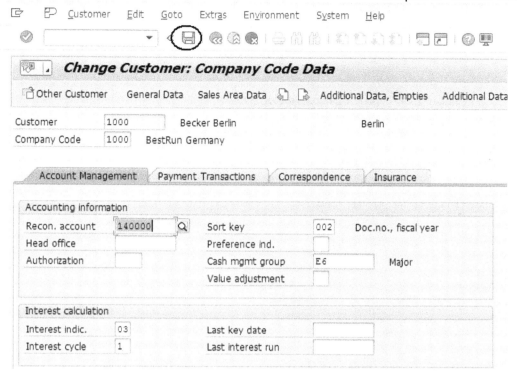

IMPORTANT: The changes will take effect once they are saved, and any document created after that will take them into consideration.

Any document created previous to the customer update will not reflect those changes.

Functionality – Display an Existing Customer

Modifying an Existing Customer	
Menu Path	SAP Menu > Logistics > Sales and Distribution > Master Data > Business Partner > Customer > Display
Transaction	XD03

To display an existing customer, use transaction XD03.

In display mode, no changes can be made to the master data, but you will be able to display all the values registered on the fields.

This is useful because in some environments, you will not have access to update the customers, but you will be able to display their data.

As with the update transaction, you will need to enter the customer number and the organizational data if you want to display information from the company code and the sales areas.

Display Customer: Company Code Data

Other Customer   General Data   Sales Area Data   Additional Data, Empties   Additional Data, DSD

| Customer | 1000 | Becker Berlin | Berlin |
| Company Code | 1000 | BestRun Germany | |

Account Management | Payment Transactions | Correspondence | Insurance

Accounting information

Recon. account	140000	Sort key	002	Doc.no., fiscal year
Head office		Preference ind.		
Authorization		Cash mgmt group	E6	Major
		Value adjustment		

Interest calculation

| Interest indic. | 02 | Last key date | |
| Interest cycle | 1 | Last interest run | |

Reference data

| Prev.acct no. | | Personnel number | 0 |
| Buying Group | | | |

This transaction displays the changes a customer master data has undergone.

This is important because there may be need to track when a particular change was made to a customer, what the original value was, and who made this change.

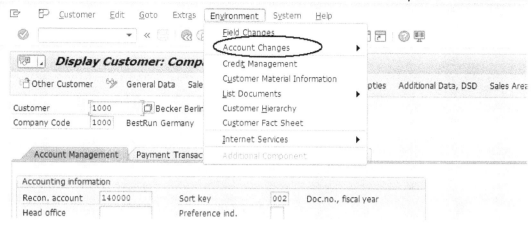

Example:

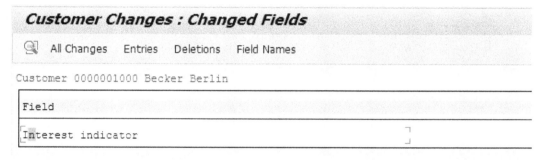

❖ Double-click on the field to see the details of the change (the new and old values).

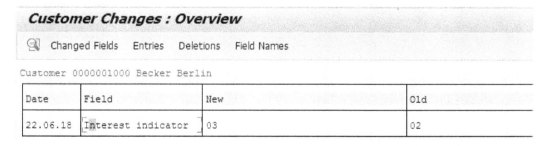

Configuration – Creating New Customer Account Groups

Creating an Account Group	
Menu Path	SPRO > Logistics General > Business Partner > Customer > Control > Define Account Groups and Field Selection for Customers
Transaction	OVT0

The account group is required to create the customer master and in the partner determination procedures.

The account group controls:

- Customer number ID (internally or externally assigned)
- If the customer will be a one-time customer or not
- Available fields (mandatory, optional, or not visible)
- Default customer pricing procedure
- Partners available

As mentioned in the functionality section (Sect 4.1.1), there are several groups available with standard SAP, and if you need to create a new one for your company, you can do this by copying one of the original ones.

In this example, we will copy a new one for the one-time customer group.

Display IMG

Existing BC Sets   BC Sets for Activity   Activated BC Sets for Activity   i Release Notes   Cha

Structure
- Flexible Real Estate Management (RE-FX)
- Logistics - General
  - Product Lifecycle Management (PLM)
  - Portal
  - Material Master
  - Quantity Optimizing and Allowed Logistics Units of Measure
  - Assortment
  - Additionals
  - Retail Pricing
  - Demand Management Integration
  - Business Partner
    - Analyze Partner Relationships
    - Identify Origin of Partner Data
    - Agreement with Other Applications re Partners
    - Work Out Quantity Framework for Partners
    - Customers
      - Control
        - Analyze Customer Master Fields and Define Field Usage
        - Define Account Groups and Field Selection for Customers
        - Define Transaction-Dependent Screen Layout
        - Define and Assign Customer Number Ranges

Example: Your Company is already operating, and you normally have an account group for regular customers.

Now, a new requirement comes to identify customers for a trade show. They will be defined as "one-time customers", and they will not be considered part of your regular customer pool.

In this case, we will copy the standard "CPD – one-time customer group" and create "ZCPD – expo one-time customer group."

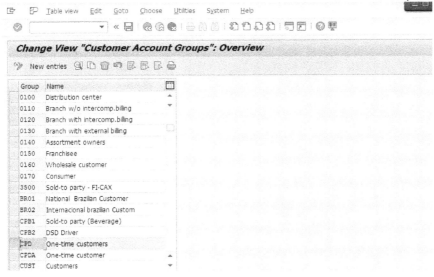

❖ After selecting the customer group to be used as a reference, select the "Copy" button, and assign the new data to the customer group.

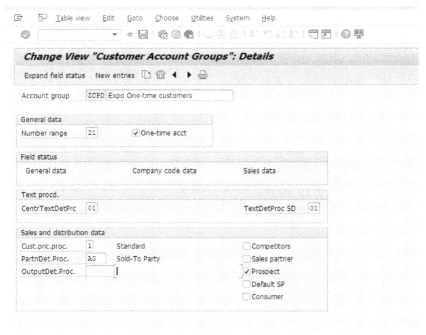

❖ Once all information has been captured, save the changes.

5.2. PRODUCTS

Uses and Functionality

Material master is a central data that is available at all levels, and contains all materials that a company procures, produces, or sells. It can include tangible materials or intangible materials (like services sold or purchased).

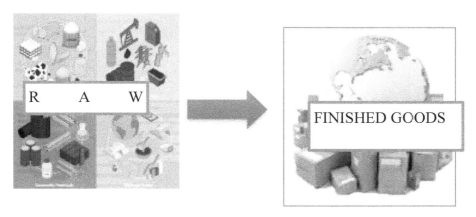

There are different material types, and they are used for several operations in the company. Examples of these include raw materials (ROH), semi-finished goods (HALB), finished Goods (FERT), packaging materials (VERP), and services (DIEN).

The configuration of the different views, material number ranges, etc. is normally covered on the Materials Management module, so those topics will not be covered in this book, and only the fields relevant for the sales and distribution functionality are included.

In this case, how to configure the material master will not be covered, but you will be shown how to create a new material, since it will be required for the exercises, as well as for your company or project.

Functionality – Create a New Material

Creating a New Material	
Menu Path	Logistics > Material Management > Material Master > Material > Create General > Immediately
Transaction	MM01

The materials can be created in two ways: the easy way and the complex one.

The option discussed in this section will describe how to create individual materials, not a mass upload for material master (there are special programs for that functionality, not covered here).

Individual materials can be created as follows:

Option A – Create a brand new material, without reference
- In this case, all the required fields will be blank and will need to be filled in order for the material to be saved and a new one created.

Note: When you start creating materials for the first time, you will need to start with this option.

It is recommended to create at least one of each material types you will use in the future, so you can use the easier and faster way with option B.

Option B – Create a new material, copying from an existing one
- In this case, all the fields from the original material are copied to the new one, and you can change whatever information needs to be updated.
- Once the required fields are filled, you can save the new material.

Note: Any changes made to the new material will not affect the original material. The source material is only taken as a reference to avoid typing repeated information.

In any case, once you determine the way you will create the material (with or without reference), you need to know how the number ranges for the materials have been set up, as you may need to enter the material ID.

Possible configurations:

- Manually assigned:
    - You determine the material ID number or alphanumeric combination, according to any logic or naming convention allowed on the system and within your company.
    - In this case, when creating the material, you need to manually assign the proper ID for the material.
    - **Examples**: FG0000001, RAW456, R2D2-C3P0. DOGANDCAT.
- Automatically assigned by the system (SAP recommended):
    - The system automatically assigns the following numeric consecutive within the material type.

Note: Different number ranges could have been created to facilitate identification of the material types.

    - In this case, leave the material ID number blank (as the system will assign the number upon saving).
    - **Examples**: 50000000000, 9000000000, 8000001, etc.

❖ Enter the industry sector most closely matching your company's and the material type, then select the enter icon.

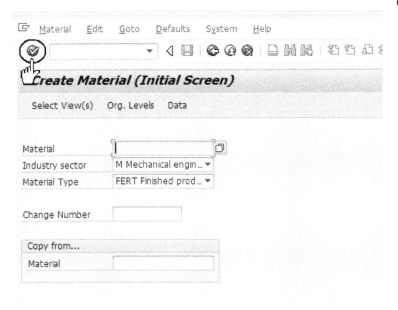

5.2.2.1. Selecting the Material Views

The material master has hundreds of fields that can be included as detailed information for the material.

Related fields are organized into groups called "views" for increased organization.

Each material type will have particular views that might not be available for other material types.

Example:

- The raw material types assume that you will normally be using these materials as part of the production process and that they will not be sold, so they do not normally have access to the sales views.

- A material that is purchased and re-sold (trading goods) assumes it will not be part of the production process, so it does not have MRP, forecasting, and work scheduling views.

- ❖ When creating the material, select the appropriate views for your material type and operations.

At the very least, a material needs the following views to be used in SD:

- Basic view
- Sales views (1, 2, and Sales/Plant)
- Accounting view
- Plant view (if stock item)
- Storage location view (if stock item)

❖ Select the enter icon.

If you will normally use only certain views, click the **Save Default Setting** icon, and the selected views will appear selected the next time you create a new material.

Note: This must be used before selecting the enter icon.

5.2.2.2. Organizational Data

After the views, you need to enter the organizational data for the material (for which plants and sales organization the material will be valid).

❖ Select the enter icon.

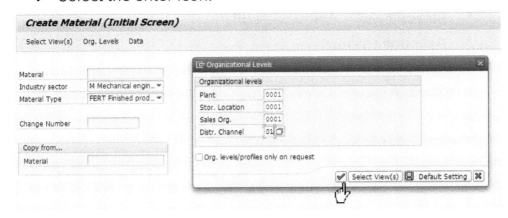

5.2.2.3. General View

The general view contains information relevant to all plants and sales areas.

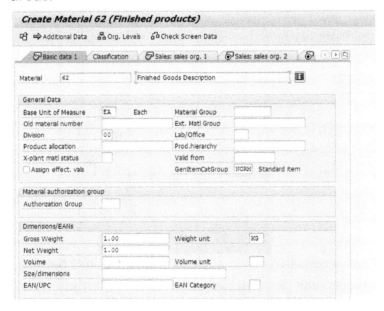

For the fields marked in yellow, a brief description is included.

Field	Use
Base unit of measure	The base unit for costing, as well as inventory tracking and inventory valuation

Division	The material can only have one division. This is part of the sales area
GenItemCatGroup	This will be used to determine the item category for the sales documents
Gross Weight	Will be used on shipping data and print outs
Net Weight	Product weight including package

5.2.2.4. Sales View 1

In Sales View 1, you can enter the basic information related to sales. This information can be unique to the sales organization/distribution channel combination, if required.

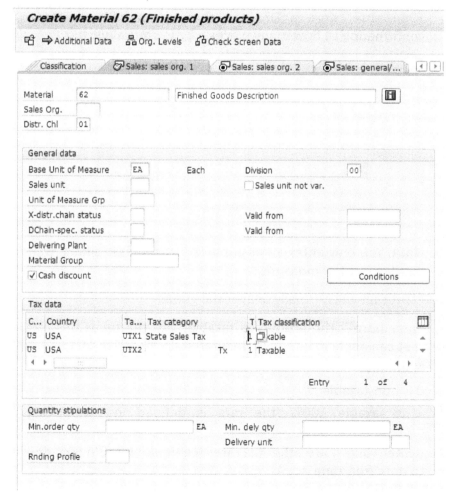

The fields marked in yellow are either required for the SD operation, or optional, but useful to know.

Field	Use
Base unit of measure	Copied from General View
Division	Copied from General View
Sales unit	Alternative units of measure for the product.
	Very useful when you have a product which you will sell on a different presentation than the base unit of measure.
	Example: The base unit of measure is EA, but this product is sold only by the dozen.
	Then enter here a DZ, and the system will ask for a confirmation of how many pieces a DZ is equivalent to.
	Note: You only enter a sales unit of measure if it differs from the base unit of measure.
Delivery Plant	Plant that will normally deliver the goods
Tax Data	Enter here if the product is taxable, and the types of taxes that can apply to it (Can be federal, state, jurisdiction, etc.)
	Normally:
	0 is non-taxable
	1 is taxable 100% (the rate is defined in the pricing procedure)
	{Other values} are other tax rates (**Example**: taxable 50% due to duty free zone, etc.)

5.2.2.5. Sales View 2

For Sales View 2, the most relevant fields are also marked.

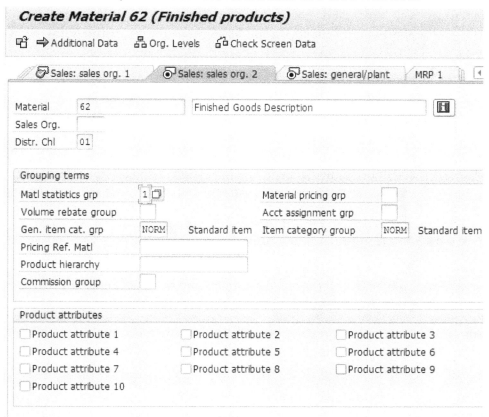

In this case, the fields for material pricing group and acct assignment group are optional.

Field	Use
Material Statistics Group	This field (in combination with the customer statistics group) will be used to accumulate the sales values for the aggregated reports on the Sales information System (SIS)
Material Pricing Group	Can be used as a parameter to determine new pricing conditions or rates **Example:** We assign the material to a pricing group "01 – Super discount" (which in this example will be my products that are about to become obsolete). Then we create a promotion with a "65% discount" on pricing group 01. As a result, all materials with this pricing group can get a discount of 65% (instead of creating a 65% discount per each material)
Acct Assignment Group	This group can be used via configuration to determine different revenue accounts for finance.
Item Category Group	The field is required to determine the item category in the sales documents
GenItem Cat Group	Only used if nothing is entered on the item category group field. If this applies then the value in this field is taken as a default.
Product Attributes 1 – 9	This field don't have any particular function, and they can be defined to any value the company requires (For pricing for example)

5.2.2.6. Sales / Plant

The Sales/Plant view is data that is related to a particular plant. The most relevant fields are as follows:

Create Material 62 (Finished products)

⊡ ➡ Additional Data 🔠 Org. Levels 🔠 Check Screen Data

| Sales: sales org. 2 | Sales: general/plant | MRP 1 | MRP 2 | MRP 4 | F. |

| Material | 62 | Finished Goods Description | 🔢 |
| Plant | | |

General data

Base Unit of Measure	EA	Each	Replacement part	☐
Gross Weight	1.00	KG	Qual.f.FreeGoodsDis.	☐
Net Weight	1.00		Material freight grp	
Availability check	02	Individ.requirements	☐ Appr.batch rec. req.
☐ Batch management

Shipping data (times in days)

| Trans. Grp | 0001 | | LoadingGrp | 0001 |
| Setup time | | Proc. time | | Base qty | | EA |

Packaging material data

Matl Grp Pack.Matls [ ]

General plant parameters

| ☐ Neg.stocks | Profit Center | | SerialNoProfile | | DistProf | |
| | | | SerializLevel | |

Field	Use
Availability Check	Review the product availability for shipping dates confirmation
Batch Management	If this is marked, it will signify that the product is handled in batches
Transportation Group	Used to group together materials that ship in a similar way (this is used later on the process for shipping)

Loading Group	Used to group together materials that are picked in a similar way (this is used for the pick-pack process)
Material Group Packaging Materials	Used to determine if the material requires a specific packaging material or sequence of packaging instructions
Profit Center	The sales from this material will be reported into this profit center (only if profit centers are active for the implementation)

5.2.2.7. Plant/Storage Location View

The information relevant to the Plant/ Storage Location view is copied from the previous screens in SD.

8. Accounting View

The Accounting view includes the following information about the material:

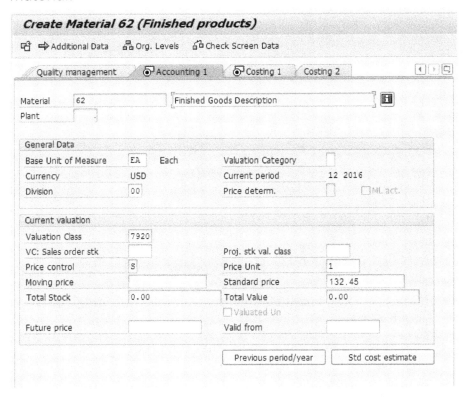

Field	Use
Valuation class:	A grouping that will determine the financial account where the stock value will be posted to
Price Control	"S" – Standard / "V" – Moving average price
Price Unit	Number of units to which the price refers Example: • 1 EA of Notebook = $1,500, then unit price is 1, Standard Price = $1,500 • 1000 EA of Chip = $10, then unit price is 1000, Standard Price = $10

Functionality – Modifying a Material

Changing a New Material	
Menu Path	Logistics > Material Management > Material Master > Material > Modify > Immediately
Transaction	MM02

The material can be modified once created if needed.

The same views available for creation can also be updated normally.

Most of the fields available upon creation time will be open to change also on modification.

However, specific fields will not be able to be modified so as to maintain consistency in the information:

Some fields not available for modifications include:

- Material number
- Price control
- Moving average or standard price (depending on the price control)

❖ To modify a material, enter the material ID, and press enter.

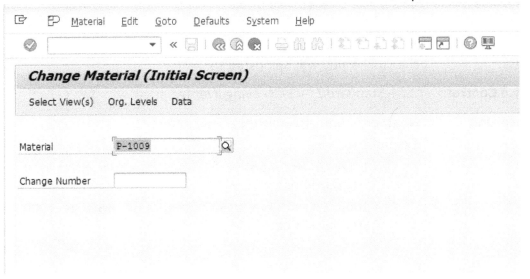

❖ After that, select the view(s) you would like to be updated.

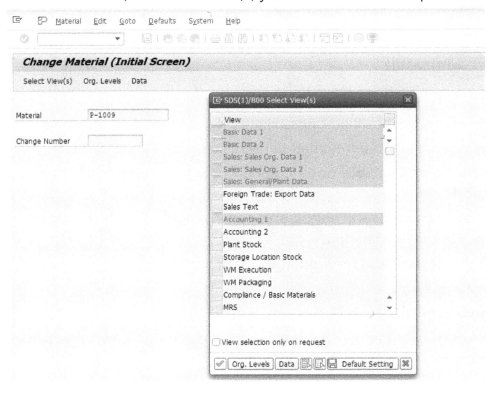

Note: If a particular view was not selected at the time of initial creation, the view cannot be modified. It will have first to be created on the "Create Material" function (MM01 – Transaction ID).

❖ After that, enter the organizational information.

If this information is not entered, you will only see available fo-
modification data that applies generally to all the different
organizational structures.

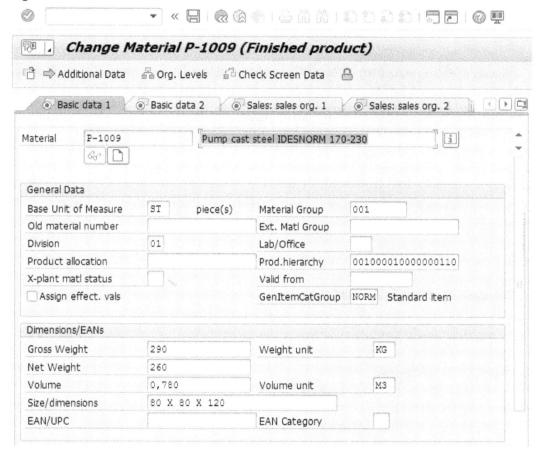

❖ After the necessary changes have been made, select the save
icon.

Functionality – Displaying a Material

Displaying a New Material	
Menu Path	Logistics > Material Management > Material Master > Material > Modify > Immediately
Transaction	MM02

In display mode, you can see all the information from the material in any of the views selected; however, nothing is available to be updated.

In many projects, most of the users have access to display the material master if required, but only a selected few will be able to update/create new materials.

❖ To display the material, enter the material number, the views you would like to display, and the organizational data.

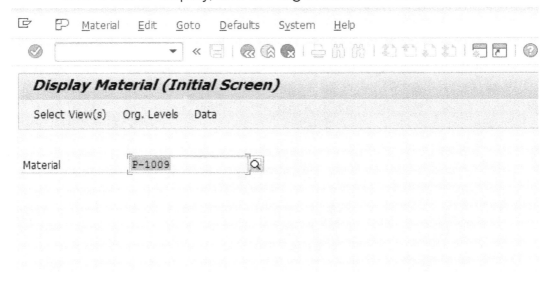

As with creation and display, you will only see the information available for the created/selected views and data.

❖ Click enter and you will be able to display the information for the material.

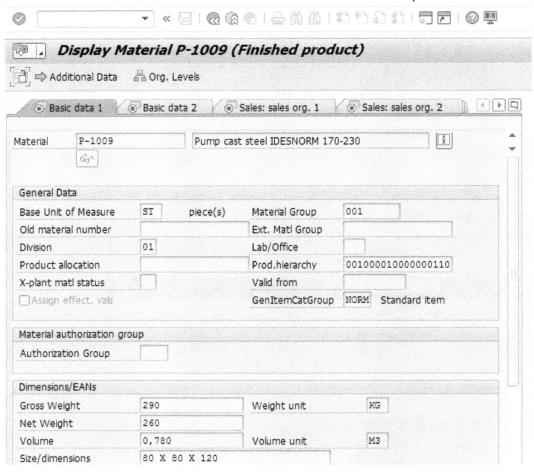

❖ To exit the display of the material, click the back button or go up on the navigation bar.

Configuration – Create a New Transportation Group

Creating a New Transportation Group	
Menu Path	SPRO > SD > Basic Functions > Routes > Route Determination > Define Transportation Groups
Transaction	N/A

Transportation groups are used in shipping to determine which materials should be grouped together for transportation.

Example: Assume there are three different products to ship. If all of them have the same transportation group, they can be included in the same delivery and shipment.

However, if any of those products has a different transportation group (i.e. needs to be refrigerated), a different delivery for this particular material must be determined.

SAP provides the following readily available transportation methods:
- 0001 – On pallets
- 0002 – In liquid form

If the available transportation groups do not meet your needs, in order to create a new one, you will need to copy one of the standard transportation groups.

❖ Select the original transportation group to copy from, and select the copy icon.

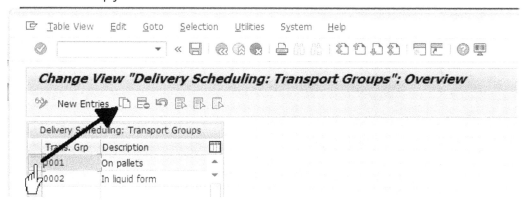

❖ Enter the new transport group ID and description.

Configuration – Create a New Loading Group

Creating a New Loading Group	
Menu Path	SPRO > Logistics Execution > Shipping > Basic Shipping Functions > Define Loading Groups
Transaction	SPRO

Similar to the transportation groups, the loading groups will help you group materials which need to be loaded together for shipping.

They will also help you to determine the shipping point.

If the loading groups available do not meet your needs, to create a new one, you will need to copy one of the standard loading groups.

❖ Select the original loading group, and select the copy icon.

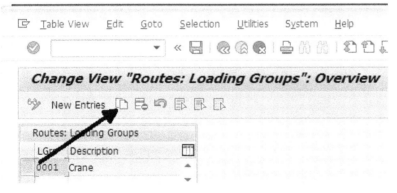

❖ Enter the new loading group ID and description.

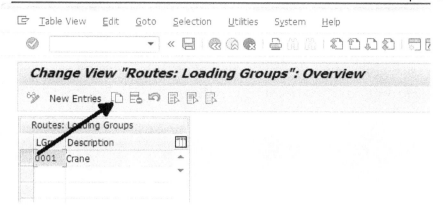

❖ Save your changes.

8.3. EXERCISES

- Create two new customers for your newly created company code and sales area (using standard customer account group)
  - ○ Customer No. 1 generated number: _____
  - ○ Customer No. 2 generated number: _____
- Create a new transportation group: _____
- Create a new loading group: _____
- Create two new materials (type FERT) for your plant and sales area.
  - ○ Material No. 1 generated number: _____
  - ○ Material No. 2 (with an alternative unit of measure for sales view): _____
  - ○ Assign to your new material the new transportation group: _____
  - ○ Assign to your new material the new loading group: _____
- Create a new customer account group (similar to the "Sold-To" group)
  - ○ New account group # _____
- Create one new customer with the new account group.
  - ○ New customer generated number: _____

6. PRICES AND CONDITIONS

6.1. USES AND FUNCTIONALITY

The pricing concept is used in the calculations of the final prices for our goods or services.

Many factors will influence the pricing, like customer price list, materials; materials price list, surcharges, discounts, etc.

Example: Imagine there are the following price elements on a company:

Product 1 (Ice Cream Cups) - Base Unit Price = $5.00, Discount on January = 10%, Taxes = 7%

If someone enters a sales order for 10 ice cream cups, our price calculation will be as follows:

Base Price = $5.00 x 10 units = $ 50.00

Discount = 10% = ($50 X 0.1) = - ($ 5.00)

Subtotal = $ 45.00

Taxes = 7% (over subtotal) = $45 x 0.07 = $3.15

Total = Subtotal + Taxes = $48.15

This section will demonstrate how the master data for prices is entered, and the configuration section will demonstrate how to create new conditions and use them for your requirements.

SAP comes with pre-defined pricing "concepts" of base prices, surcharges, discounts, etc. called "condition types."

Included here is a list of the most commonly used conditions. With these minimum conditions, you would be able to set up a basic pricing schema.

Condition	Description	Type	Calculation Base
PR00	Base Price	Price	Fixed
IV00	Intercompany base price	Price	Fixed
HD00	Freight	Surcharge	Fixed
MWST	Taxes	Taxes	Percentage
HB00	Fixed discount	Discount	Fixed
HA00	% Discount	Discount	Percentage

For each one of the conditions, there are several different ways of determining the price.

- Fixed value: The price is directly entered
- Based on distance: **Example**. $0.40/mi.
- Based on weight: **Example**. $1.00/lb.
- Formula based: Calculations are done to determine the final price for this particular condition

All these concepts are grouped on a calculation procedure that includes all the steps the system must follow to reach the final price.

The basic and most common calculation procedures are already defined in the standard system, and they are enough to start working with them.

6.2. FUNCTIONALITY — REGISTERING A NEW PRICE

Registering a New Price	
Menu Path	Logistics > Sales and Distribution > Master Data > Conditions > Select Using Condition Type > Create
Transaction	VK11

The functionality to enter a price, discount, or surcharge will allow you to register a new pricing condition for your products or services.

❖ Select the concept (condition type) you want to enter the price for and select the enter icon.

In this example, you will see how to enter the base price of the material.

After this, the possible combinations (access sequences) will appear to enter the price.

❖ Choose your desired combination and select the enter icon.

Note: In this example, you can enter the base price based on the following examples of each of the combinations:

Key Combination	Example	Price	Comments
Customer / Material	Material 1234 / Customer ABC Material 1234 / Customer XYZ	$25.00 $28.00	Normally used if a few combinations are used or if a specific price is given by exception to a particular customer
Price List / Material	Price List 01 / Material 9876 Price List 02 / Material 9876	$120 $150	This price list will be associated to the customer, so all customers that belong to the price list 01 and buy material 9876 will get a price of $120, while customers that buy the same material, but have price list 02 will get a price of $150
Material	Material 4567	$99.99	This will apply to all customers

It is possible to have information for the same material on all three combinations, and depending on the configuration, the system could include the three prices on the calculation or stop at the first option.

Whenever possible, try to create the prices at the most general level (via groupings, price lists, etc.). Otherwise, the data maintenance becomes a very cumbersome task to maintain.

Imagine your company has 500 items to sell and 100 customers.

If you want to maintain prices at customer/material level, then you will need to maintain prices for 50,000 records.

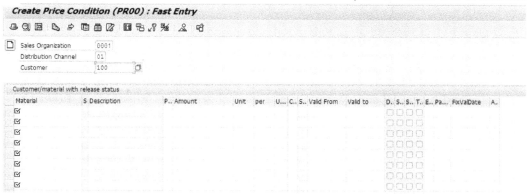

For this example, you need to enter the sales organization, distribution center, material, and the following data: amount, unit, per, unit of measure, and validity dates.

Note: The validity dates are very important, since the price calculation will take the price in effect at the price date.

Example: $1,000 USD (From 01/01/2016 – 05/30/2016)

             $1,500 USD (From 06/01/2016 – 12/31/2016)

If we enter an order on 06/01/2016, the system will not find a valid price.

If we enter an order on 06/02/2016, but we indicate to the system that the price date will be 05/30/2016, the price will be taken as $1,000 USD.

It is not possible to enter two price records for the same combination with different dates on the same transaction. If you want to enter different prices for the whole year (like in our previous example), you will need to enter them one at the time, repeating VK11 with the different validity dates.

The following additional functionality is available:

Button	Function	Button	Function
	Displays the header information for the conditions		Shows the details of the condition, as well as if there are any limits, and how the condition is calculated (fixed value, based on distance, etc.) **Example**: We can have a price per km.
	Additional data for the condition		Scales You can enter different prices according to a scale value. Example: 1 – 1 dz = $25.99 dlls 13 – 100 = $20 dlls 100 – 1000 = $18.99 Over 1000 = $16.50
	Condition supplement Additional conditions (discounts, surcharges) that will be applied automatically whenever the current pricing condition is active		Validity periods Allows adding a range of dates and prices for these dates. Let's assume we sell a "Drone" Example: High season (Nov – Jan) = $100 Medium season (Feb – Jun) = $95 Low season (Jul - Oct) = $93
	Free goods Will allow entering free goods whenever the registered condition applies. **Example**: We sell drones, and every time a customer buys 1 item, we will give them a "USB memory". Then we will enter the code for a this material as a free good		Condition text Additional texts that can be added for the condition. Later on, these texts can be printed out if needed

Button	Function	Button	Function
	Information about the condition status **Example**: The condition can be pending to be released, and therefore not yet active		Conversion factors which indicate the conversions between the units of measure **Example**: Material is handled in EA, but we enter a price per case. We will need to enter a conversion factor: 1 case = 250 EA
	Key What are the "Key" combinations for this conditions		Cumulative order values (or billing values) Shows the values for all sales orders or billing documents that have used this condition
	Shows an overview of the condition records		

Functionality – Modifying an Existing Price (Condition Record)

Registering a New Price	
Menu Path	Logistics > Sales and Distribution > Master Data > Conditions > Select Using Condition Type > Update
Transaction	VK12

To modify an existing condition record, use transaction VK12.

In this transaction, you will be able to update the condition prices.

If the change being made is a new permanent value for the base price, discount, or surcharge, it is recommended to use the "create" functionality, as you can create a new price for a different day.

This will allow you to keep track of all the price changes through time.

The "update" functionality is available, but it does not keep track of the changes made to the condition type.

❖ For this change, you will need to know the condition type and the validity date you desire to update. Enter them and click enter.

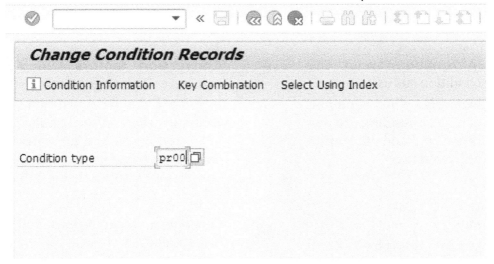

❖ After this, enter the key combination for the price.

Note: If you need to update the condition in the different options, you will need to repeat this operation for each one of the possible key combinations.

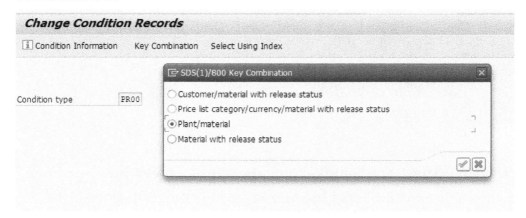

❖ Once you select the appropriate combination, click enter.

❖ On the following screen, enter the corresponding information.

Some information will be mandatory and will need to be registered to be able to continue with the price update.

Also, the validity date is important, as there could be different prices according to the date.

Example:

You could have a regular price of $100 for the past year.

For the current year, the price will change to $105.

If you need to change it to $105.5- for this year, you will need to enter a date within the new validity date.

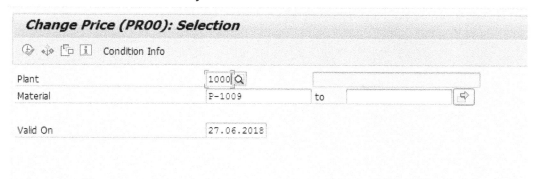

Functionality – Displaying an Existing Price (Condition Record)

Registering a New Price	
Menu Path	Logistics > Sales and Distribution > Master Data > Conditions > Select Using Condition Type > Display
Transaction	VK13

To display an existing condition record, use transaction VK13.

❖ For this information to be displayed enter the condition type (price, discount, etc.) and click enter.

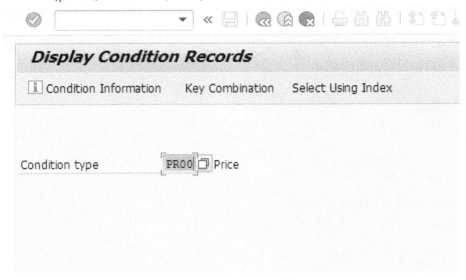

❖ After that, select the combination you wish to display the prices for.

❖ Once you have indicated the condition combinations, register the information, entering the mandatory fields.

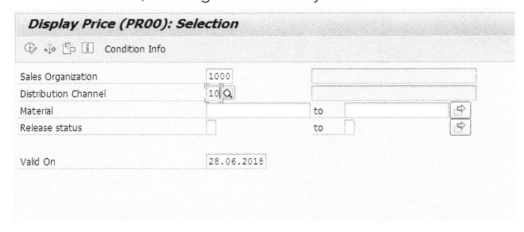

❖ After entering the required data and the validity date, select the button.

You will see all the prices entered for the particular combination

On this screen, you will be able to display the information for the prices.

IMPORTANT: This list and information cannot be downloaded directly to file. If you need the information for your records, the following section will indicate how to obtain a price list.

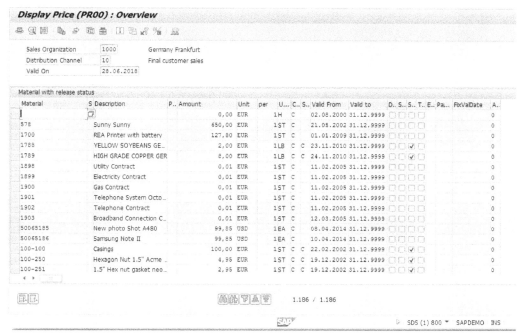

The information in the first columns will vary according to the key combination selected.

To the right, the following columns are standard independently of the key combination selected:

- Calculation type: How the price is calculated (percentage, fixed amount, formula, etc.).

- Scale basis: How the scales (if the product has them) are based (value, weight, quantity, etc.).

- Valid from: Indicates the date when the condition price starts being "active".

- Valid to: Indicates the date when the condition will finish being "active".

Note: If the price is entered on a date not within the validity date, the price will not be included in the calculations of the final price on the sales documents (sales orders, invoices, etc.).

- Deletion: If the column is marked, the particular condition is marked for deletion.
- Supplements: If the column is marked, the condition has "supplemental" conditions.

Note: Condition supplements are additional conditions linked to this particular condition. If this condition is applied, all the other conditions are automatically applied also.

- Texts: If the column is marked, the column has long text stored.
-

6.3. CONFIGURATION

The pricing configuration is one of the most important and complex processes on sales and distribution, so the logical process will be covered in detail.

Once you understand how SAP determines the prices, you can follow a similar procedure for other determination processes like account determination, text determination, printer determination, etc.

The procedures will be covered from the simplest to the most complex elements:

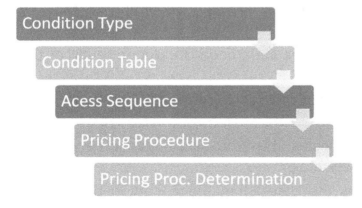

Configuration – Condition Type

Menu Path	SPRO > SD > Basic Functions > Pricing > Define Condition Types > Maintain Condition Types
Transaction	SPRO

First, all the possible concepts that will compose the final price must be determined, including base price, surcharges, discounts, and taxes. Almost all concepts that affect the price will require a specific condition type.

Imagine that each one of those concepts is included on a spreadsheet on an individual row. In SAP, each one of these possible concepts will be created as a "condition type." By default, SAP has pre-installed the most commonly used condition types for use.

As a general practice in SAP, if you need to modify a standard condition or fine-tune it to meet your needs, it is always best to copy it and create a new one.

In this example, you will create a new discount. A store gives discounts for birthdays depending on your age; you get a discount of your age divided by two.

❖ First, create a copy of one of the standard discounts.

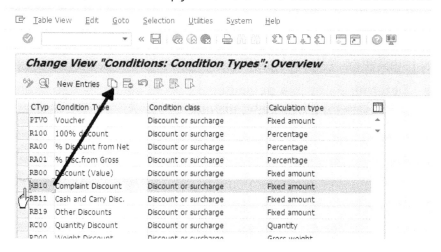

The new condition type will be ZBRD – Birthday discount:

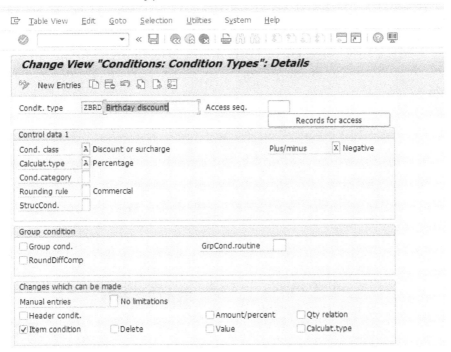

Field	Use
Access Sequence	How the condition type will be processed (if nothing is included, then it is assumed the user will enter the condition manually)
Condition Class	Use for the condition (surcharge, base price, tax, rebate)
Plus/Minus	If the condition is a discount/surcharge. Use negative if will always be a discount, and positive if it will always be a surcharge. If it can be both, then leave blank
Calculation Type	Determine if it is a percentage, a fixed value, or based on other criteria (like weight, distance, etc.)

Changes Can Be Made	Define the types of changes that can be made to the condition when the user is entering the sales order. For security reasons, commonly, the conditions that are determined via a price list are defined as "not modifiable". In this way, the user registering the sales order cannot manually change the price.
	In the "Manual Entries" field, you can also have a condition that is determined by the price list, but override it manually (in this case, manual condition has priority)
	If the condition is fully modifiable, then all checkboxes must be marked as such.
	If you expect only certain changes to be available, then mark the corresponding areas that can be changed (percentage, value, if it can be deleted, etc.)

Normally, we distinguish between standard transactions and those newly created by us by initializing them with "Z", or "Y" (if you run out of "Z" combinations)

Configuration – Condition Tables

Creating a New Condition Table	
Menu Path	SPRO > Basic Functions > Pricing > Pricing Control > Define Condition Tables > Create Condition Tables
Transaction	V/03

You need to define a condition table to determine the combination of fields that will be used later in the access sequence. SAP provides as standard several combinations of the most commonly used fields, but you are free to define any combination you require from the available field catalog.

Note: It is possible to include additional fields not defined in the field catalog, but this require ABAP, which is not in the scope of this book.

First, determine the table number you will use for your new table (as a convention, newly created tables usually start in the range of 900).

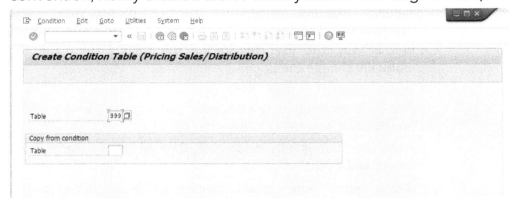

❖ Then, select the fields that will form your table by double-clicking on each one of them.

You need to first enter the header field, and then enter the ones that will be a "detail" field.

If you want to offer a specific discount for a particular sales office (for example, for our north region, we will offer a 10% discount, but for our south region, we will offer a 15% discount to boost sales in that region), then you will need to differentiate them by the sales office.

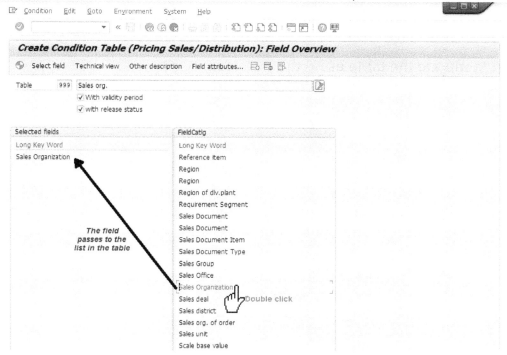

Note: If you need to know the technical field names (some fields are very similar in their description), you can click on "Other description," and it will toggle between different descriptions (short description, long description, technical and short description, etc.). You can select it until you find the description more suited to your needs.

❖ Once you have all your required fields, you can confirm with the Technical View which fields were defined as key fields and which are in the detail.

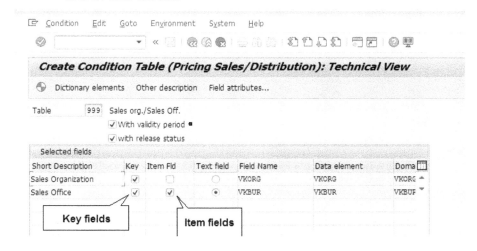

❖ Once you have confirmed the key fields and item fields, you can generate the table using the ⊕ icon.

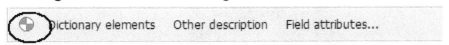

The system will confirm if you want to generate the table (answer YES). Since this configuration is a "Workbench" definition (you are creating a new table in the database), and not a regular customization, it will ask you for the package and other attributes. Your basis/ABAP team can provide this.

❖ Once you provide the information, you can save the table, and it will generate a new transport number.

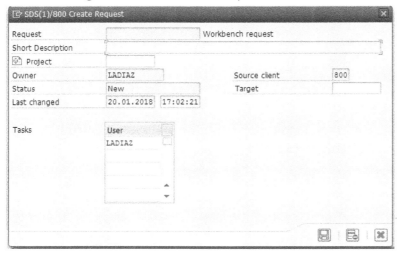

This is what is given after the information is saved and the table is generated.

❖ Once created, return to display the table, and it will appear on the list of available tables to select.

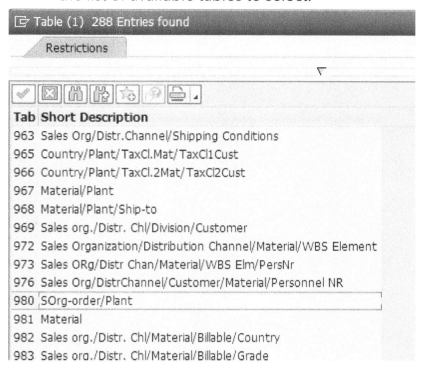

At this point, nothing else is required to configure the condition table.

Configuration – Access Sequence

Menu Path	Sales > Basic Functions > Pricing > Pricing Control > Define Access Sequence > Maintain Access Sequence
Transaction	SPRO

In the access sequence, as its name implies, you define the sequence with which you will access information for the pricing condition. It is normally recommended that the access sequence go from the most specific condition to the most general.

Example: If you have one access with only sales organization, it should be after "Sales Organization / Distribution channel / Material / Customer."

This is done to optimize performance, as for every condition type in your document; the system normally does a search in the condition tables for all your access sequences trying to find the correct price.

❖ In order to create a new access sequence, you can select it from the main folder and select the copy icon.

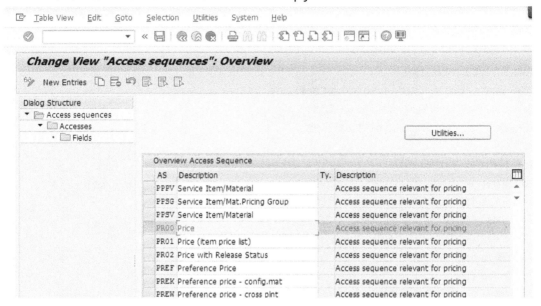

❖ When selecting the option, you will get a message asking if you wish to copy all the dependences and information. Select **copy all.**

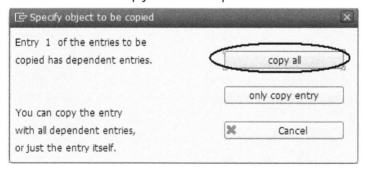

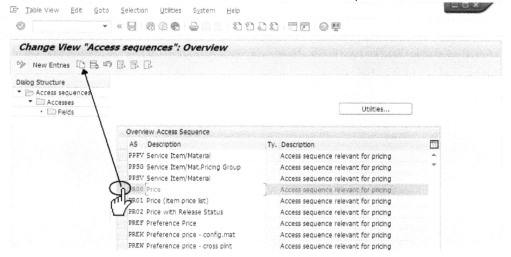

❖ After copying, select the "Accesses" folder to get the detail of the tables included.

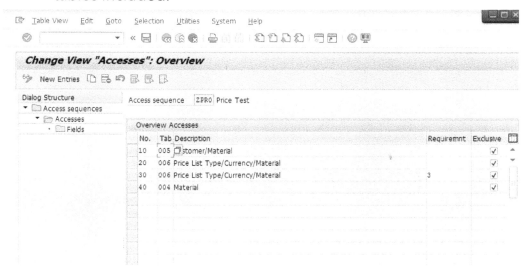

In this case, let's assume our table is more general than the number 20. Normally we would create our accesses in the order in which they should be searched for, and usually with numbers in multiples of 10. This is done because in the case that one table needs to be added later on, there will be enough room to insert it where it belongs without altering the desired search order.

To add your table, select "New entries", and include the step number and the table number you wish to add, select the enter icon, and select the green arrow to return to the list of all available access for the sequence.

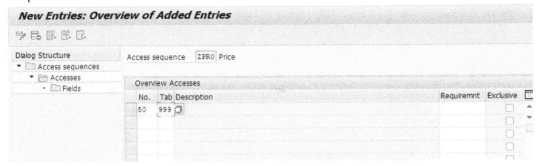

Your table should appear now in the list of available accesses in the table.

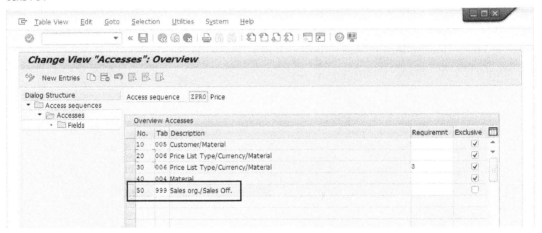

Once your table is on the list of accesses, you will need to confirm the fields from that table.

❖ Select the step and open the "Fields" folder.

Note: The first time you access the fields; the system might give you a message stating that the field assignment has not been made. This is standard message, so select the enter icon to continue.

❖ Make sure there are no errors on the assignment.

Note: If all fields are in green, you are good to go!

Upon saving, this will also be a workbench request, separated from the configuration.

```
Prompt for Workbench request                                    [X]

View Cluster Mainten...  VVC_I682_VA

Request              SR3K900208        [ ] Workbench request
Short Description     New Condition table

                           [✓]  [&°][⊟][D][ Own Requests ]  [✕]
```

Configuration – Pricing Procedure

Creating a new Pricing procedure	
Menu Path	SPRO > SD > Basic Functions > Pricing > Pricing Control > Define and Assign Pricing Procedures > Maintain Pricing Procedure
Transaction	SPRO

Once you have defined your condition tables, access sequences, and condition types, you can create (or update) the pricing procedure. Think of it as the sequential order in which the system processes the information for each one of the condition types. In it you can also include subtotals and store some of the values in specific variables that can be used in further calculations.

This pricing procedure can also include references to additional formulas, as well as conditions that need to be met for a condition to be included in the final price calculation.

To define it, again the recommendation is to copy an existing one and modify according to your needs. For SD, the standard most commonly used is RVAA01 – Standard.

❖ The first step is to select the desired pricing procedure to be copied, and then select the copy icon.

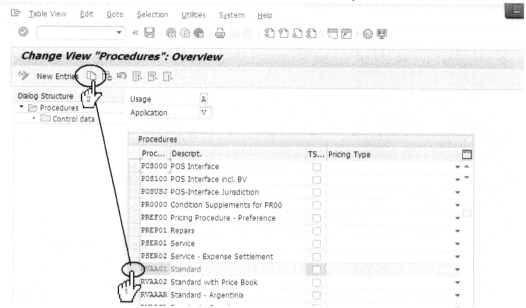

❖ Enter the new ID and description of your pricing procedure and select the enter icon.

❖ On this screen, you will get a message asking if you want to copy all the entries and dependencies or only the entry. Select **copy all**.

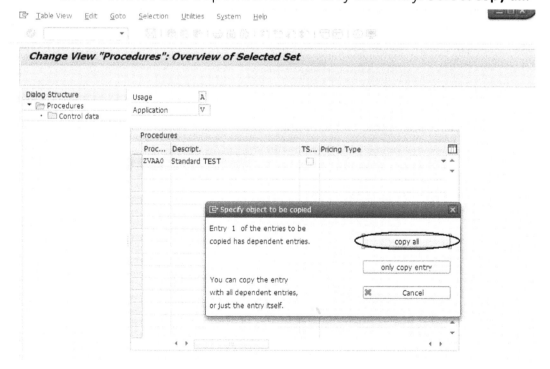

In this case, all entries, condition types, and requirements will be copied.

❖ If you get the following message, select the enter icon to bypass it.

⚠ You should use the counter only for manual item conditions

Then, select your new pricing procedure and open the folder for Control data, where you will enter all your condition types.

In the pricing procedure, you will group your conditions normally for base prices, and then include any additional price (surcharges) or discounts, plus any other charges (i.e. freight, taxes, rebates).

A line in the pricing procedure represents a subtotal with no condition type associated.

The pricing procedure will be determined for each combination of sales order and customers (see Pricing Procedure Determination in the next section).

Note: All the condition types to be used on a document must be included in the pricing procedure (even conditions that will be entered manually at a given time).

Note: The pricing procedure normally follows sequential steps, from the top down.

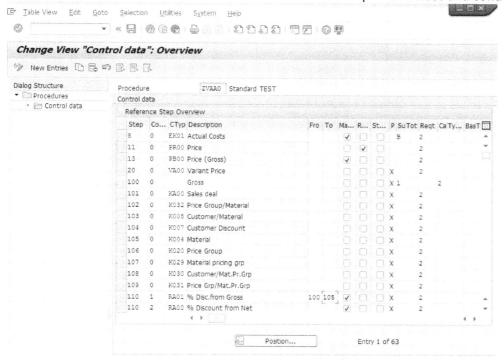

Be careful when updating or deleting pricing procedures.

If you change an existing pricing procedure associated with documents previously generated, any changes made to the procedure will be reflected in the original sales order, and this may cause inconsistencies between the sales order and the invoice.

Note: The accounting documents of any previously posted invoices are not affected by this change, but if you go to display the invoices, they will reflect the changes and will not match with what was posted. Avoid this by creating a new pricing procedure and determining it for newly created documents.

The following table contains a detailed description of the columns included in the pricing procedure:

Field	Use
Step	The sequence the system will follow to determine the final price. It is a common practice to create the steps in multiples of 10 (for simple pricing procedures). For very complex procedure, you can include increments of 5 or 2. **Note**: This is done to leave room for adding condition types later on if an additional calculation is required.
Counter	Normally is left blank. For a complex procedure, you can define sub-steps within a particular step, so you can have additional room for adding condition types. **Example**: Step 10, counter 1, 2, 3, etc.
Condition Type	List of all condition types that will be allowed in the document. A blank represents a subtotal for the pricing procedure.
From	Initial number for the range of conditions to consider. You need to include the step number. In the previous example, step 110 includes everything from line 100 (adding the gross price and any other discount or deal from 101 to 105). **Note**: The "From" can normally be from conditions that are above the current line.
To	End of the range for the conditions to consider. You need to include the step number. In the previous example, you have the last condition to consider on 105.
Manual	Indicates if the condition will be manually added in the document. If it is marked, it will not appear automatically, and the user will need to manually add it.
Required	Indicates if the condition is mandatory. **Example**: Taxes (even though the rate is 0%, the condition still needs to have a value determined).
Statistical	Indicates if the condition is statistical. Means that the condition will be calculated for informational purposes, but will not be taken into consideration for the final price calculation.

Field	Use
Print	Indicates if the condition detail can be included on the printed documents.
Subtotal	Indicates if the subtotal will be stored on one of the available variables. This variable can be used for further calculations later on, so this becomes a powerful ally whenever you have a very complex pricing schema.
Requirements	This indicator represents what conditions need to be fulfilled for the condition type to be active. If the conditions for the routine are not met, then the condition will not be activated. **Note**: This routines are defined in transaction VOFM, via ABAP code. **Example**: For discounts, Routine 2 validates that the item has a price.
Calculation Type	This represents an alternative calculation formula for the condition. These formulas are defined also in transaction VOFM via ABAP. **Example**: You can count the number of items included on the sales order and depending on that, give a certain discount percentage.
Base Type	This allows you to include a specific calculation base for the condition. **Example**: Assume you included your subtotal gross price in Subtotal 1 (KZWI1). Now you want to have the following calculation: Condition value = Gross subtotal KZWI1 * 0.22 Your condition can have the value of 22%, and it will multipy for KZWI1.
Account Key	This indicates the account group where the condition type will post to. In account determination (to be seen in the SD Advanced Configuration book), you will use this key to determine the final account to be used.

Field	Use
Account Key for Accruals	If the condition will be considered an accrual for an expense (or a revenue) that will be collected later, then enter the corresponding key.
	In account determination (to be seen in the SD Advanced Configuration book), you will use this key to determine the final account to be used.

Configuration – Pricing Procedure Determination

Creating Pricing Procedure Determination	
Menu Path	SPRO > SD > Basic Functions > Pricing > Pricing Control > Define and Assign Pricing Procedures >
Transaction	SPRO

To determine a pricing procedure, there are two elements: the customer pricing procedure and the document pricing procedure. The combination of both is what will determine the procedure to be used in the sales document.

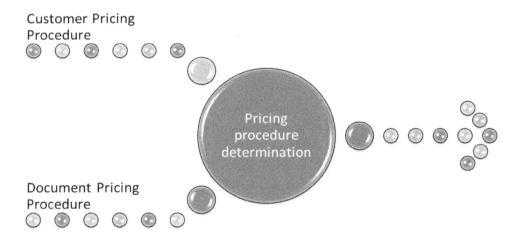

Customer Pricing Procedure

Document Pricing Procedure

6.3.3.1. Customer Pricing Procedure

First, you need to define the customer pricing procedure:

Path: Define customer-pricing procedure (within the path for pricing procedure determination).

You need to select **New Entries** and add the customer procedure ID and description.

Note: In this configuration step, the only item to perform is to create the ID and its corresponding description. This information will be used when creating the customer master in master data creation.

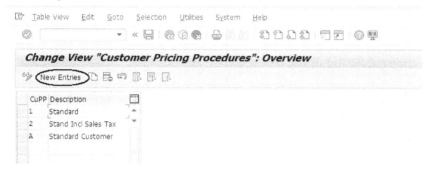

❖ After entering this data, save the changes.

6.3.3.2. Document Pricing Procedure

First, you need to define the document pricing procedure:

Path: Define document-pricing procedure (within the path for pricing procedure determination). Select **New Entries** and add the document procedure ID and description.

Note: In this configuration step, the only item to perform is to create the ID and its corresponding description. This information will be used in customizing when creating/maintaining a document type.

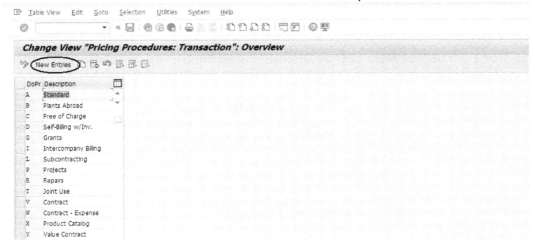

❖ After entering this data, save the changes.

6.3.3.3. Assign Document Pricing Procedures to Order Types

Once you have defined a document pricing procedure, you need to assign it to the document type (for sales orders). You can do so on the following path:

Assign document-pricing procedures to order types (from the pricing procedure determination). For each one of the sales order types you have, it is required to assign a particular pricing procedure ID.

Note: Several pricing procedures can have the same procedure ID, but with additional combinations (like customer procedure ID), it could be possible to determine a different pricing procedure.

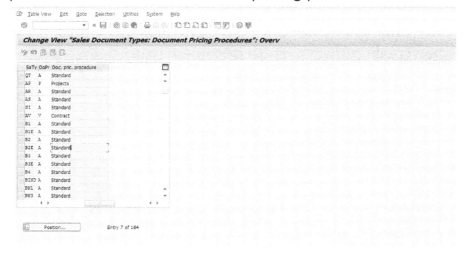

6.3.3.4. Assign Document Pricing Procedures to Billing Types

In a similar way that pricing procedure ID is assigned to a sales document, it also needs to be assigned to a billing document.

Note: It is important to be consistent with the document procedure ID assigned in the sales order, because if you determine a very different pricing procedure, you could end up with two different prices for the sales order and the invoice.

If the pricing will be maintained from the sales order to the billing type, it is possible to skip this assignment or leave the billing type ID blank.

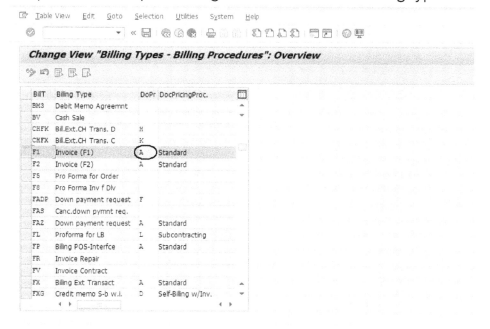

6.3.3.5. Define Pricing Procedure Determination

After the customer pricing procedure and document procedure have been created, you can define the combinations that will help you to determine the final pricing procedure to be used. This can be done in the following path:

Define pricing procedure determination (within the Pricing Procedure Determination section). The factors that can derive a different pricing procedure are:

- Sales organization
- Distribution channel

- Division
- Document pricing procedure
- Customer pricing procedure

Example: For the same sales organization/distribution channel/customer/ documents but different division, you could have two (or more) different pricing procedures. If you find a combination similar to what you will be determining, you can use it as a reference to copy. The condition type included in the pricing determination is a default pricing condition that will appear in the input for conditions automatically when creating the documents.

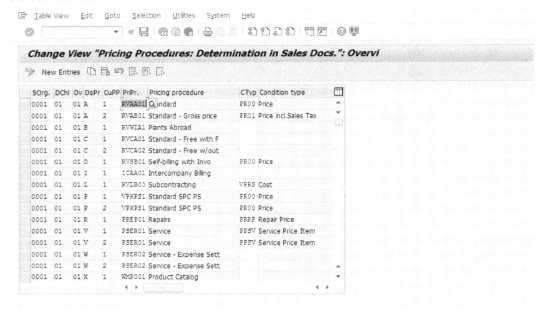

7. SALES DOCUMENTS

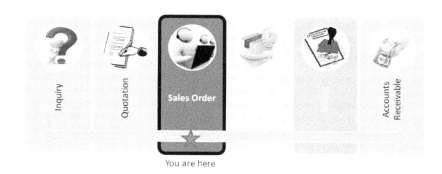

You are here

7.1. USES AND FUNCTIONALITY

This chapter will focus on the main sales process once it is time to enter a sales order.

The sales orders in SAP start the process of "order to cash" (The inquiry and quotation are optional documents, not required to start the process).

They represent an order from the customer to deliver the company products or services.

Different from an inquiry or a quotation, which normally are not considered for production planning, a sales order is considered a "firm" document, normally legally binding.

 This document will trigger (if necessary) the creation of new production orders and future documents like deliveries and billing documents.

All sales documents are composed of:
- Header: Information that applies to the document in general (**Example**: Payment terms.)
- Items: Information that applies to each one of the materials/ services to be sold. (**Example**: Prices, texts, etc.)
- Schedule lines (only in particular cases, like inquiries, quotations, and sales orders): A list of all possible delivery dates/times for each one of the items.

For the header, just as we have customer or material groups, we have independent functionality depending on the type of sales order.

The first operation is to create the sales document with the appropriate type.

In standard SAP, there are already several document types defined, which will perform different functions depending of the selected document type.

The document type for a sales order will determine the number range, as well as visible, mandatory, or hidden fields, and allowed follow-on functions.

In standard SAP, there are approximately 30 different document types already pre-defined and ready to be used (if they are marked as allowed for your particular sales area).

The most common document types are:

ID	Description	Common Use
OR	Standard Order	To sell products, services. A delivery document needs to be generated for goods issue. After delivery, an invoice will be generated.
SO	Rush Order	To sell products and services. The user does not have to create the delivery, as it is created manually. The invoice can be created right after the sales order has been created.
RE	Returns	To process returned products to your company. After goods are received, a credit memo can be created.
CR	Credit Memo Request	To process credits that need to be posted to the company's clients. This is the request, and after that an actual Invoice (credit memo) is generated. Normally goods are not involved. **Example**: You need to credit your customer $100USD per incorrect price.
DR	Debit Memo Request	To process credits that need to be posted to the company's clients. This is the request, and after that an actual Invoice (credit memo) is generated. Normally goods are not involved. **Example**: You need to charge your customer an additional $100USD for each damage to your containers.

Functionality – Creating the Sales Order

Creating a New Sales Order	
Menu Path	Logistics > Sales and Distribution > Sales > Order > Create
Transaction	VA01

You will first see how to create a sales order, the starting point for your process, and describe the components of it. Later on, you will see the fundamentals of configuration and note important areas to watch.

❖ First, enter your data, including order type and the sales area (sales organization, distribution channel, and division) and select the enter icon.

The order type is what does the magic to determine how the document will behave. The document type can differentiate between a regular sales order, a rush order, and a returns order.

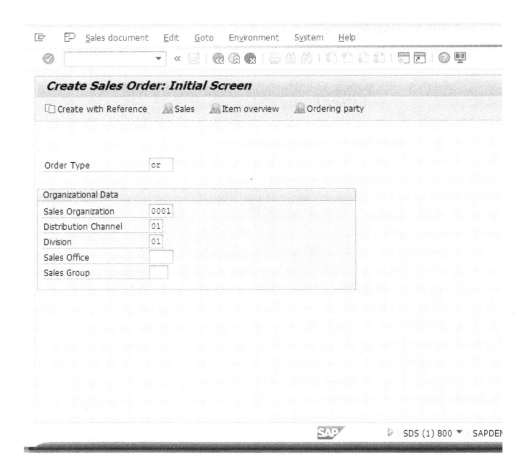

After this, you will see the main screen for creating a sales order.

7.1.1.1. Header

❖ First, enter the information in the header.

Important fields include:

Note: Most of them are mandatory.

ID	Common Use
Sold-To	Customer sold-to – To whom are we selling?
Ship-To Party	The address where we will ship to. If several are available, a screen will pop out to select the desired ship-to address – To whom are we shipping the goods?
PO Number / Date	The PO the customer sent to request the goods (if applicable) / date when the PO was sent.
Req. Deliv. Date	The general date when the customer wants the goods delivered.
Pricing Date	The reference date for pricing.
Payment Terms	The terms of payment agreed with the customer. They came by default from the customer master, but can be changed manually here if necessary.
Incoterms	Print on the shipping documents. Can be used to calculate prices and surcharges on the sales order.

7.1.1.2. Items

❖ Next, enter the items.

The items contain the detailed information for each material or service the organization is selling.

Each position will also have a particular "item category" (type), which determines additional functionality.

Example: If the item should be copied to the delivery, if it is a text position, if it is relevant for pricing, etc.

The most important fields are:

ID	Common Use
Material	Material Identification Number
Order Quantity	Order quantity
Amount	Total amount. Can be entered manually if not available prices to calculate

In some cases, you will enter an internal order or a WBS element (for project-related sales order). At header level, you can see the detailed information for the document. The information entered here applies to all the items on the sales order.

Note: On the right side of the screen, you can see the menu to move around each one of the views (each folder tab is called a view).

On all SD documents, there is a text section, where you can capture text that will be printed out on the documents (invoice, shipping documents, etc.). Other texts are only for informational purpose or notes regarding the sales order.

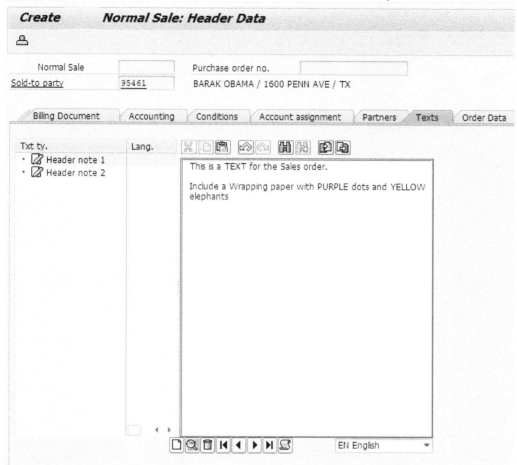

This is how it will look once the main information is filled out.

Please note that in this example, for the third item, the material description was changed from the original description entered on the material master.

This is allowed and used for some cases when a sporadic (or express) sale is needed and the material/service are not available, or when selling something that is a one-time deal. For regular situations or sales that will repeat over time, it is not recommended and it is a best practice to create the corresponding material master.

Create   **Normal Sale: Overview**

Orders

Normal Sale		Net value	906.40	USD
Sold-To Party	95461	BARAK OBAMA / 1600 PENN AVE / TX		
Ship-To Party	95461	BARAK OBAMA / 1600 PENN AVE / TX		
PO Number		PO date		

Sales | Item overview | Item detail | Ordering party | Procurement | Shipping | Reason for rejection

Req. deliv.date	D 10/07/2016	Deliver.Plant	
☐ Complete dlv.		Total Weight	0.00 KG
Delivery block		Volume	0.000
Billing block		Pricing date	10/07/2016
Payment terms	0024 Payment Due Net 30		
Incoterms	FOB		
Order reason			
Sales area	/ 01 / 07		

All items

Item	Material	Or...	ItCa	Net price	Net value	Amount	Un	Order	S	Description
10	9001967	1.00	ZTAD	226.60	226.60	100	EA		☐	Material description 1
20	9001968	1.00	ZTAD	453.20	453.20	2443	EA		☐	Material descrption 2
30	9001967	1.00	ZTAD	226.60	226.60	434	EA		☐	My changed material description if neede

If you want to see the detailed item information, you can select it a particular line and click on the details icon at the very bottom of the screen.

There are additional buttons with the following functionality:

Button	Function	Button	Function

	See details (either at header or item level)		Add new lines to the sales order to capture additional items
	Delete a line item **Note**: This can be done only if no deliveries or invoices have been posted for the item		Move to item number **Note:** This is very useful if you have a sales order with a large number of items
	Select all items		De-select all items
	Triggers availability check		Display availability
	Shows the schedule lines (per item) The schedule lines are the dates when the system calculates the goods will be available for shipping and the system can confirm the order		Pricing Shows the detailed pricing for a particular items (base price, discounts, surcharges, taxes)
	Triggers batch determination, if the product is handled in batches **Note**: The automatic batch determination is an advanced functionality where the system can propose the product batches to be used at delivery time, and this will be sent to the warehouse for product picking and shipping		Items detail: configuration This is an advanced functionality used for configurable materials only

This is the detailed information that is available for the item.

Note: On the right side of the screen you can see the menu to move around each one of the views (each folder tab is called a view).

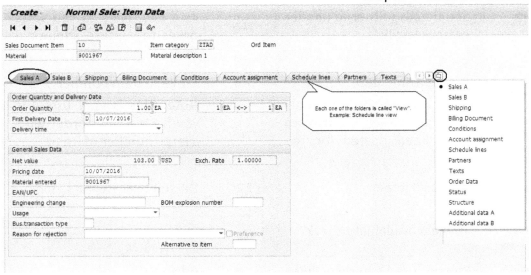

This is what can be seen in the detailed pricing view.

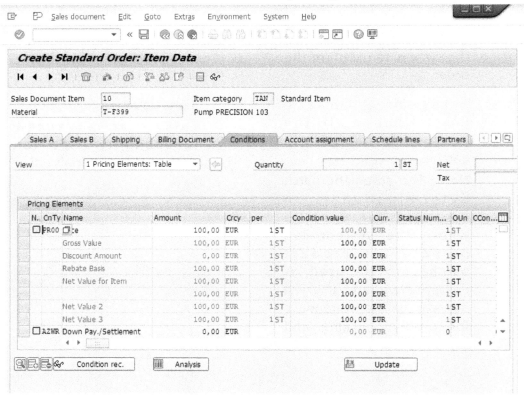

7.1.1.3. Schedule Lines

On the schedule lines, you can see the required quantity from the customer, as well as the confirmed quantity in the system.

If the whole quantity cannot be confirmed for a particular date, then the system will create a new line with the confirmed quantity.

Normally, the schedule lines are entered automatically by the system.

However, you can manually include or modify existing schedule lines according to your business needs.

❖ After entering all required data on the sales order, save it.

Functionality – Order Status and Document Flow

Displaying Document Flow	
Menu Path	Logistics > Sales and Distribution > Sales > Order > Display
Transaction	VA03

At any given time after creating a sales order, you can know its genera status by changing the display and showing the document flow.

In this transaction, you can see the complete history of the sales documents, as well as all documents linked to it.

The next figure shows the documents following the sales order.

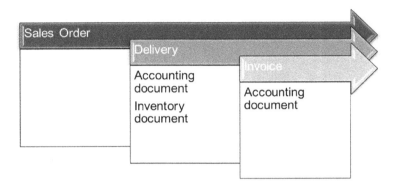

❖ On the main screen for display (or change) or within the detail of the sales order, select the icon for Document Flow to see the order status.

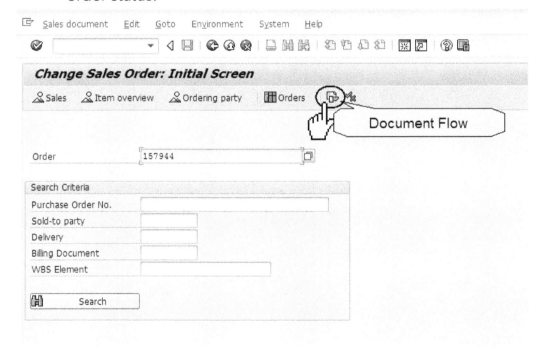

This will show the general status of the order.

In this case, there are two invoices related to the order, but one of them was cancelled, so the order is partially invoiced. Once all items are completed, the order will show as completed.

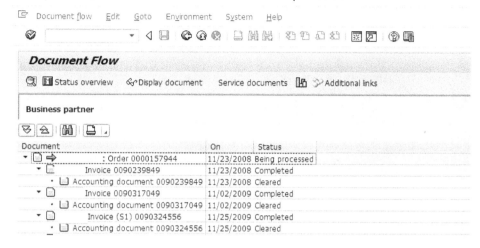

Note: If you go to the details of the order and select an item, you will see the status for that particular item.

In this example, you can see how the sales order appears as complete for item 10.

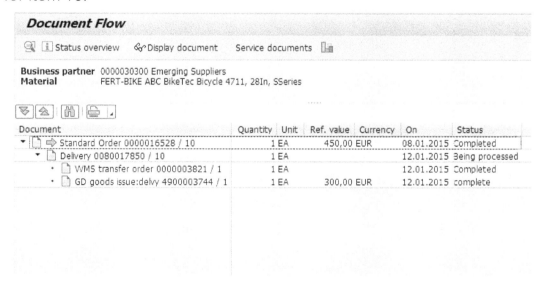

Functionality – Modifying a Sales Order

Modifying a Sales Order	
Menu Path	Logistics > Sales and Distribution > Sales > Order > Modify
Transaction	VA02

❖ Enter the document number of the sales order to modify and select the enter icon.

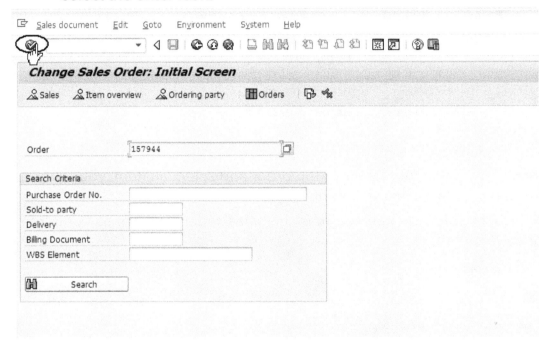

This will show the fields open for update.

If you do not have subsequent documents, almost all the fields are available for modifications.

On the other hand, if you have already created deliveries and billing documents related to this sales order, some fields will not be open for modification, as this could create inconsistencies in the information created.

In this case, you will receive a message like this:

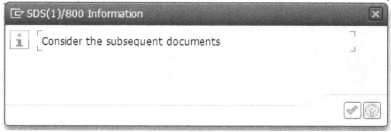

❖ To close it, press enter or click on the green check mark.

In the following screens, you can update the fields available for modification.

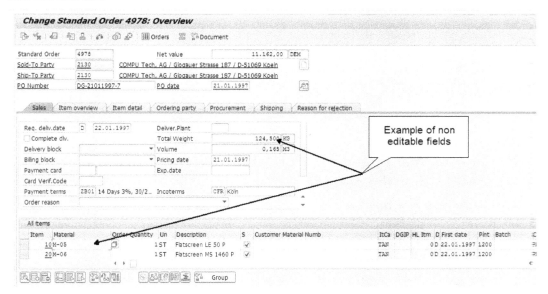

In the update mode, if changes have been made to pricing, they will not reflect automatically.

❖ For this, manually select the "re-calculation" button, so the prices can be read again.

❖ To execute this option, select the item you need to update, and the "condition" prices.

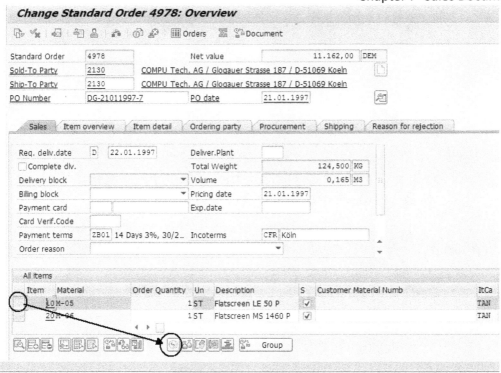

❖ Once on that screen, click on "Update" (if available) to take into consideration the new prices.

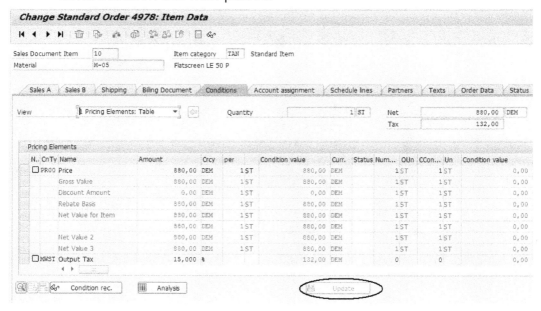

❖ After making the required changes, save the document, to get your updates registered.

Functionality – Displaying a Sales Order

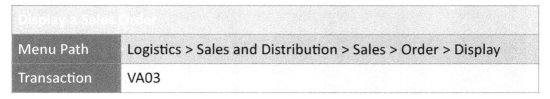

Display a Sales Order	
Menu Path	Logistics > Sales and Distribution > Sales > Order > Display
Transaction	VA03

❖ Enter the document number of the sales order to display and select the enter icon to continue.

On this screen, you can display the sales order, but you cannot make any changes to it.

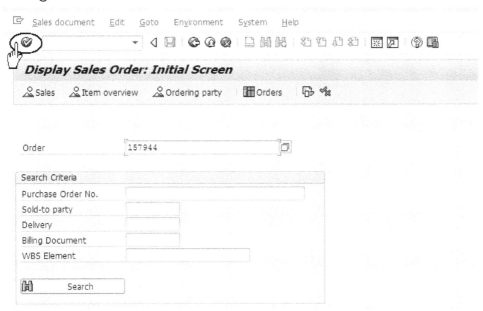

You will be able to display the information, prices, etc.

From this screen, you can also see the changes made to the document through time.

❖ Select from the main menu (Environment > Changes) and you will see a new screen where you will be able to get the report for the changes list.

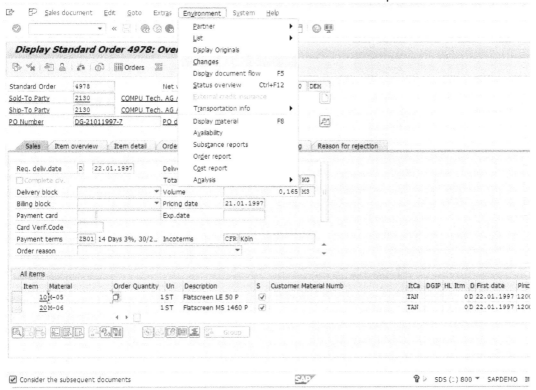

In here, you will get the parameters, which will allow you to see all the changes applied to the document.

❖ Click on the "Execute" button or press the function key F8.

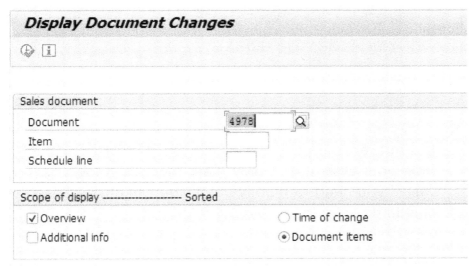

You will see a list of the changes.

Changes in Order 4978

Choose

Changes in Request 0000004978

ID	Date	Item	SLNo	Sales Promotion	User
☐	29.06.2018			Customer purchase order number changed	LADIAZ
☐	29.06.2018	10		Item credit price changed	LADIAZ
☐	29.06.2018	10		Profit Center changed	LADIAZ
☐	29.06.2018	20		Item credit price changed	LADIAZ
☐	29.06.2018	20		Profit Center changed	LADIAZ
☐	29.06.2018	30		Item credit price changed	LADIAZ
☐	29.06.2018	30		Profit Center changed	LADIAZ
☐	29.06.2018	40		Item credit price changed	LADIAZ
☐	29.06.2018	40		Profit Center changed	LADIAZ

❖ To exit the screen, use the "back" or "cancel" buttons to return to the original display screen.

7.2. CONFIGURATION

This section will detail the configuration required to create a new document type or its components, including item categories and schedule lines.

Recommended practice for sales documents configuration:

It is not recommended to delete the standard documents from your system, but only mark them as "blocked." This way, if you need to modify them, you can always have the standard configuration as your reference.

If you need to customize one of the existing documents, the recommendation is to create a new document type and copy from the closest document type available.

Note: It is important to reference an existing document type when you create a new document, since there are many configuration steps related to this that can be sped up by copying.

Configuration – New Document Type

Creating a New Document Type	
Menu Path	SPRO > Sales Documents > Sales Documents Header > Define Sales Document Types
Transaction	SPRO

Once the basic organizational structures, as well as partner determination has been defined, in the case you need to define a new document type, you can reference an existing one and modify it accordingly.

Note: SAP provides standard sales document types, and, as with all things SAP, it is best to try to use these whenever possible.

❖ Start by selecting an existing document and copying it. You need to enter at least the new document ID and its description.

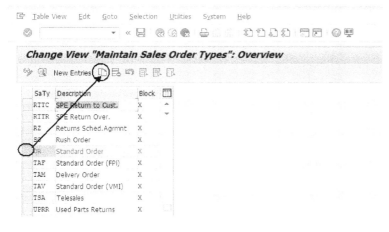

❖ After this, go into the details of the new document and modify the different options.

Note: Many of the options in this section determine the behavior for the document, what it will be able to do as well as its influence in shipping and billing, so be aware of this when changing to meet any requirements.

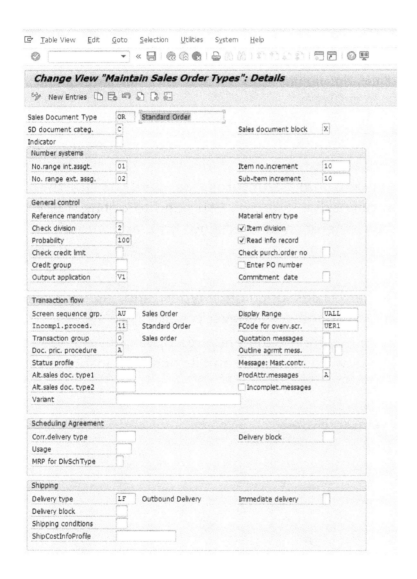

Billing

Dlv-rel.billing type	F2	Invoice (F2)	CndType line items	EK02	
Order-rel.bill.type	F2	Invoice (F2)	Billing plan type		
Intercomp.bill.type	IV	Intercompany Billing	Paymt guarant. proc.	01	
Billing block			Paymt card plan type	03	
			Checking group	01	

Requested delivery date/pricing date/purchase order date

Lead time in days		☑ Propose deliv.date	
Date type		☐ Propose PO date	
Prop.f.pricing date			
Prop.valid-from date			

Contract

PricProcCondHeadr		Contract data allwd.		
PricProcCondItem		FollUpActivityType		
Contract profile		Subseq.order type		
Billing request	DR	Check partner auth.		
Group Ref. Procedure		☐ Update low.lev.cont.		

Availability check

Business transaction	

SAP

The following table shows the uses of the main fields used for customizing a document type:

Field	Use
SD Document Category	Indicates if the document is a sales document, a quotation, inquiry, or credit or debit memo.
Sales Document Block	Indicates if the document is blocked.
	Note: In some implementations, the customer wants to see only the documents related to its operation and not see the rest on the transactions. It is not recommended to delete the standard SAP, but mark it as blocked. If you mark the document as blocked, it will not appear as available and you will not have the possibility to use it.
	On standard reports like sales document list VA05N; it will appear as available for the filters.
Number Ranges	Internal – the sales document number is assigned automatically by the system.
	External – the document number is indicated manually for the document.
	Note: This can be useful when creating sales documents from external systems and wanting to maintain the document number.

Field	Use
Increment	How your item numbers will be coded. **Example**: 10, 20, 30, etc. Can be changed to 1, 5, etc. **Example**: Item 1, 2, 3 or 5, 10, 15, etc. **Note**: The default is 10.
Reference Mandatory	You can force a document to always have a reference to another document. **Example**: A document type ZOR will need to have a reference to a quotation. Typically, credit memos and debit memos can reference an existing invoice.
Check Division	If a division at item level can be different from the division at header level.
Check Credit Limit	Only activate if you are going to be using credit management (check credit level for the customer).
Credit Group	Required for credit management functionality.
Item Division	Only mark if you want to use the division of the material in the documents (if this is allowed per the "Check Division" field).
Read Info Records	If you are using the functionality of info record (customer/material relationship), activate if you want the information existing there to be used on the sales order.
Check Purchase Order Number	If active, it will check if the purchase order number exists for the same customer, and it will stop the document creation if it finds it already in the system.
Enter PO Number	Activate if you want to make the purchase order input mandatory.
Output Application	Used for printing (V1 is always for sales orders documents).
Screen Sequence Group/Display Range	Normally used "AU" / UALL.

Field	Use
Document Pricing Procedure	Required to determine the pricing for the document. Please see Chapter 5, for additional details on pricing determination.
Scheduling Agreement	Corrective delivery type: indicates the delivery type to use when making corrections for the scheduling agreement.
Shipping	Delivery type: indicates the default delivery type to use when creating the delivery from a sales document.

Field	Use
Immediate Delivery	Indicates a delivery will be created automatically upon saving the sales order **Note**: This is normally used on scenarios like a rush order. If this is not indicated, the delivery document must be created manually.
Shipping Condition	Indicates the default shipping conditions to use while creating the delivery document.
Billing	<ul><li>Delivery-related billing type: indicates the standard invoice type to be created after the delivery of the goods.</li><li>Order related billing type: indicates the standard invoice type for an invoice created directly from the sales order (which will not be delivered).</li></ul> **Example**: for services orders.
Billing Plan Type	If the document is going to be used with a billing plan (annual, monthly billing, etc.)
Lead Time	Number of days it will take to process goods.

Configuration – Item Category

Creating a New Item Category	
Menu Path	SPRO > SD > Sales Documents > Sales Document Item > Define Item Category
Transaction	SPRO

As mentioned in the functionality for sales documents, they are formed of header, items, and schedule lines.

Just as the header has a document type, the items also have a particular type, which is called the "item category".

The item categories will group the items, and will influence the behavior of the line item.

Example: Some item categories are relevant for inventory management, but others are not. An item category can indicate the need to calculate prices, while for others this might not be necessary, as in the case of free goods functionality.

Once the document type has been defined, a new item category can be defined.

Note: It is not always necessary to create a new document to determine a new item category (and vice versa).

In the item category there are also a new set of fields that will determine how the documents will behave. As mentioned in the sales document types, SAP also provides a series of document item categories by default that normally cover the standard functionality. It is recommended to use one of the existing ones as a reference and copy it (looking for the ones most closely related to your requirements).

Examples:
- TAN – Standard for delivered items
- TAD – Standard for service items
- REN – Standard for returns

❖ To create the item category, select an existing category and select the copy icon. Once defined, enter the ID and description of the item category. After this, modify the parameters according to your needs.

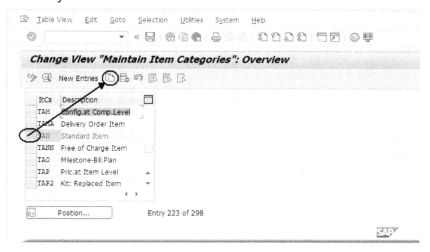

The following table explains the most common parameters used in this configuration.

Field	Use
Item Type	Leave blank if used for a standard item.
Business Item	Indicates if the data entered can be different from the header.
Schedule Line Allowed	Indicates if the item can have a schedule line associated.
Special Stock	Indicates if the item will be used with special stock.
Item Relevant for Delivery	Indicates if the item is relevant for delivery.
Billing Relevance	Indicates if the item is relevant for billing. **Example**: You might have a text item that you do not want to be included on the invoice, so you mark this item as not being relevant.
Returns	Indicates if the item is going to be used to process a return.
Weight/Volume Relevant	Indicates if you want the system to require that weight and volume be entered and considered for the following operations.
Pricing	Indicates if the item is relevant for pricing.
Credit Active	Indicates if the credit check is available/required for the item.
Statistical Value	Indicates if you want the item to represent only an statistical value rather than be included in the total value of the document. **Example**: Item 1 – $100, Item 2 – $100 (statistical), Item 3 – $100, Total value = $200 (it does not consider Item 2 for the total)
Automatic Batch Determination	Indicates f the batch determination will be run automatically upon document creation.

Configuration – Item Category Groups

Creating a New Item Category	
Menu Path	SPRO > SD > Sales > Sales Document Item > Define Item Category Groups
Transaction	SPRO

This section discusses how to define a new item category group.

Item category groups, as the name implies, allow you to group the different item categories.

They are included in the material master and can be used to determine the item category (based on the configuration).

In the item category group, you only need to determine the ID and description.

SAP provides the standard item category groups for the common operations:
*   NORM – For materials/operations that are delivered normally
*   DIEN – For services that will be included in the delivery
*   NLAG – For services that will not be included on the delivery

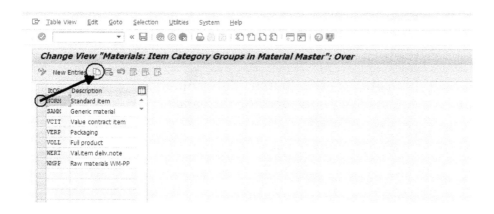

❖ Once you have the new item, you need to enter its ID and the description, select the enter icon, and save your changes.

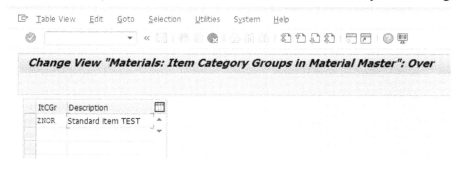

Configuration – Assign Item Categories

Creating a New Item Category	
Menu Path	SPRO > Sales Document > Sales Document Item > Assign Item Categories
Transaction	SPRO

Once you have defined the new item categories and item categories group, you can assign the allowed combinations:

- Sales document type
- Item category group
- Usage – normally is left blank unless a special use is determined
- High level item category – normally is left blank unless you are using a sub-item

From these combinations, you can automatically determine the default item category.

Note: SAP allows four additional alternative item categories to be determined that can be changed manually by the user at the moment of the entering the documents. These additional item categories must be coherent with the document type and item category group used.

Example: You will not assign an item category that requires delivery to an irrelevant sales document.

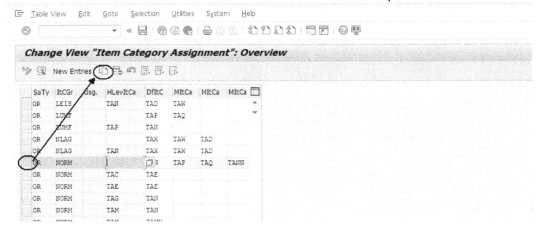

Configuration – Schedule Lines

Creating a New Item Category	
Menu Path	SPRO > Sales > Sales Document > Schedule Lines > Define Schedule Line Categories
Transaction	SPRO

The third component of the sales documents is the schedule line.

The schedule line contains information related to delivery such as delivery dates, information about the requirements transfer, and inventory management.

This element also indicates the movement type to be used at delivery time, as well as if availability check is to be done at the sales order, and if the quantities included in the sales order are to be included as a requirement for production.

First, you need to determine the schedule line category that is appropriate for your requirements. SAP provides several standard categories that can all be used to speed up the implementation process. The most common ones are:

- CP – MRP related
- CN – No material planning
- CD – Without delivery

- DN – Returns

If none of the available schedule lines matches your requirements, or you need to generate a new one to differentiate operations, you can do so by copying an existing one and changing the parameters, as needed.

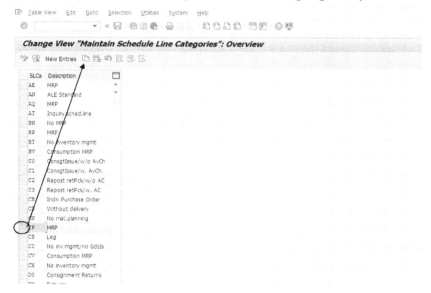

Once you have copied the schedule line, you need to verify the details of the new one to make sure the parameters entered are correct.

The table below explains in detail the main parameters for configuring the schedule line.

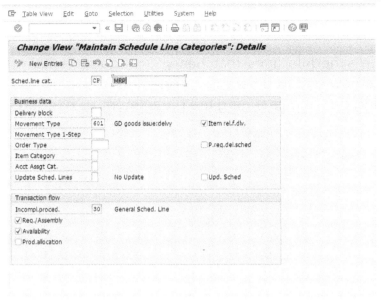

Field	Use
MVT Type	Indicates the MM movement type that will be posted whenever the delivery goods issue (or goods receipt if it is a return movement).
Item Relevant for Delivery	Indicates if the item will be relevant for delivery.
Movement Type 1 Step	Indicates if the movement will be posted in one or two steps (for stock transport orders = stock transfers between plants/companies)

If the movement is in one step, then once the stock goes out of the shipping company, the stock gets automatically transferred to the receiving company.

If the movement is in two steps, then when the stock goes out of the shipping company, the stock is moved to stock in transit, and then after it is physically received on the other site, the goods receipt is posted. |
| **Order Type** | This is the purchase order or purchase requisition. It will be used if the movment in SD will automatically generate a PR. |
| **P Req Delivery Schedule** | Indicates if the movement will generate a purchase requisition, or if it will need to regenerate the schedule for the PR. |

Item Category	Indicates if the operation will be standard (normal stock) or with a special category (consignment, subcontracting, etc.).
Account Assignment Category	Indicates if the operation will be assigned to a special account indicator (project, asset, cost center, etc.).
Update Schedule Line	This is to be used for scheduling agreements orders.
Req/Assembly	Indicates if the requirements are going to be transferred for planning. **Note**: If this is off, the sales order quantity will not be considered in the requirements.
Availability	Indicates if the item is going to have availability check verified.

Configuration – Assign Schedule Lines

Creating a New Item Category	
Menu Path	SPRO > Sales > Sales Document > Schedule Lines > Assign Schedule Lines
Transaction	SPRO

Once the indicator for the schedule line is created, you need to make the assignment to the item category and the MRP type for the material.

This combination will allow you to determine automatically a schedule line for each item that will require it.

The standard combinations are already defined in SAP, but in case you need to determine a new combination to for the appropriate schedule line, you need to make the following configuration:

❖ Select an existing combination (similar to what you need), and copy it.

The most commonly used combination is:

• TAN (Normal products) || MRP type = Blank = CP Schedule line

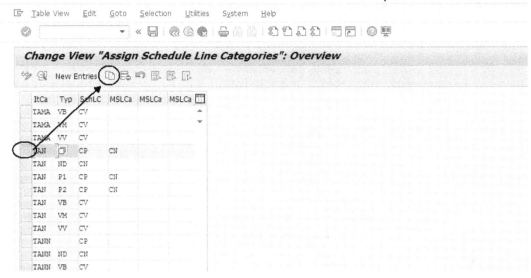

Configuration – Number Ranges for Sales Orders

Number Ranges for Deliveries	
Menu Path	SPRO > Sales and Distribution > Sales > Sales Documents > Define Number Ranges for Sales Documents
Transaction	VN01

In this transaction, you will define the available number ranges for the sales order.

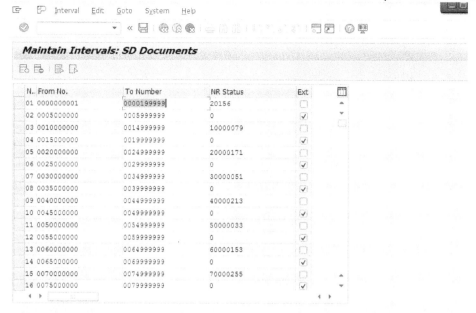

Each sales order document created is identified on the system with a unique ID number.

There are two types of number ranges: internally assigned by the system and externally assigned.

The most commonly used is the internal option, where the system keeps track of the consecutive numbers, and with each new sales order created, the interval is automatically updated.

The externally assigned number is normally used if you are using an interface where you want to maintain the same reference number in both systems.

Another reason to use an externally assigned number is if there are any business or legal requirements to identify the sales order.

All of the original documents from SAP are normally already assigned to an existing interval. It is common practice to separate groups of sales orders in different intervals, as this will tell you just by looking at the number of the document whether it is a sales delivery, a return, or a stock transfer.

IMPORTANT: The number ranges are non-transportable, which means you will have to re-create them in each environment. In a new implementation project, this will be part of the "manual" activities on the cutover plan.

For an already productive environment, the system will have to be open for customizing for the time you are doing the changes.

❖ Select the "Edit intervals" option. In there, you can edit an existing range, specifying from which number to which number the range will cover. For internally assigned ranges, there is a column called "NR Status – Number range status," which tells you the most up-to-date document number within that range.

The "To-Number" cannot be lower than the "NR Status number" for automatically assigned ranges.

The option "Ext" indicates if the range will be internal or external. If it is external, meaning you will need to manually indicate the document number, then click the check box to ON. Otherwise, you need to leave it OFF.

It is not recommended to create intervals too granular, as this will reduce the available numbers you will have for each interval, especially if you are implementing in a company with a high transaction volume. By doing this, you run the risk of running out of available numbers in an interval and needing to create a new interval, assign it to the documents, etc.

IMPORTANT: The number ranges are shared between sales orders, deliveries, and invoices. It is not common practice to assign the same interval to different document types.

Example: Sales order Type OR with interval 01, Delivery type DL with interval 01 → NO

8. DELIVERY

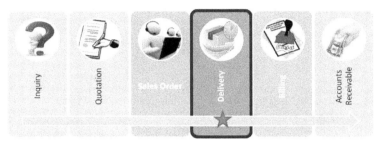

You are here

8.1. USES AND FUNCTIONALITY

Once the sales document has been created, the shipping process can begin (for documents that require a delivery).

In this process, warehouse personnel can prepare to pick the goods, pack them (if applicable), and prepare them to ship.

Also at this time, any documentation that needs to be printed out will be generated (see Chapter 9 for specific details on printing forms).

Once the goods have left the company premises, the goods issue is posted, and the inventory counts are updated to reflect this.

SAP already provides the most common delivery types required for operations. For example:

- LF – Standard delivery
- LR – Returns delivery
- NL – Replenishment delivery (for stock transfer orders)
- NLCC – for Cross company delivery

This chapter will explain the process for creating a new delivery document, without the more complex process of picking (with warehouse management), or packing (with handling units), as this is not in the scope of this book.

Functionality – Create a New Delivery Document (Individually)

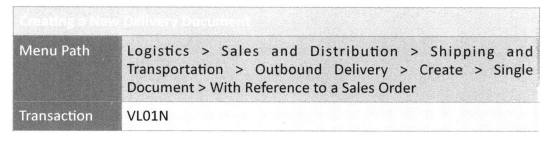

Creating a New Delivery Document	
Menu Path	Logistics > Sales and Distribution > Shipping and Transportation > Outbound Delivery > Create > Single Document > With Reference to a Sales Order
Transaction	VL01N

In this transaction, once you have completed the sales order, you can proceed to dispatch it with the delivery document. This is the transaction to process an individual document (one at the time). This can be used at any time in conjunction with the mass delivery processing.

In this case, we need to capture the shipping point and the order number.

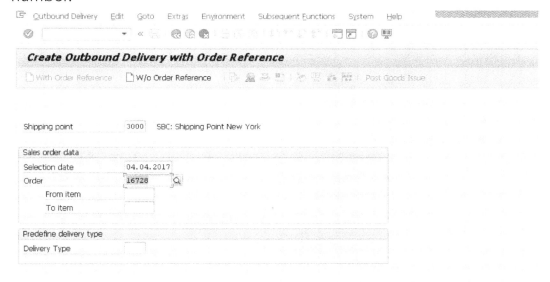

❖ After this, select the enter icon. The main screen for the delivery document will appear.

If your materials are normally not handled by batches, you will only need to enter the quantity for each one of them. If one (or several) of your products are managed in batches, you will also need to enter the corresponding batch number (or numbers) to fulfill the whole quantity.

❖ After confirming the quantity, enter the plant/storage location.

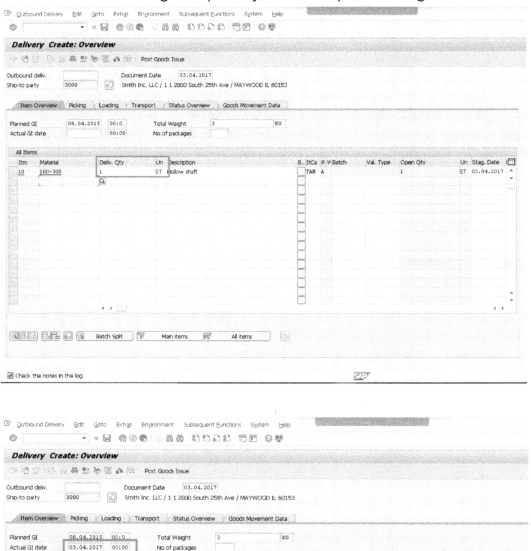

❖ In some cases, the delivery will need to be picked, and you can do so under the picking tab by entering the real quantity picked from the warehouse. Once you enter the picked quantity, the status will change from "A – Not Yet Processed" to "C – Fully Picked."

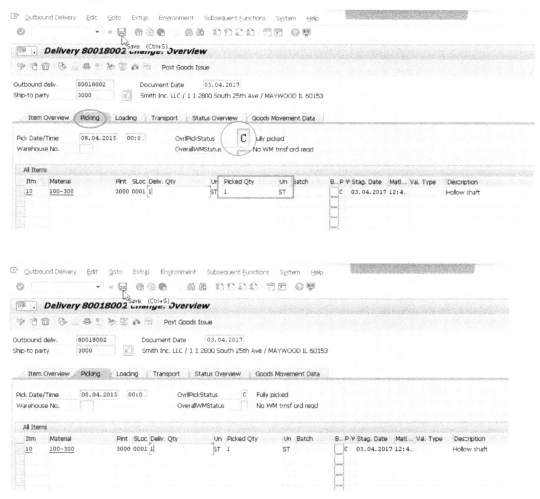

❖ Once this information has been entered, you will need to post the goods issue. You can do so by selecting the **Post Goods Issue** button in the menu:

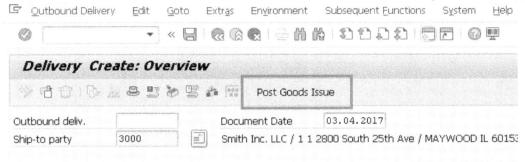

This will save the document and also deduct the inventory for the corresponding quantity entered in the delivery document.

For sales orders that require delivery, only after the post goods issue has been completed, they can be invoiced. In the case of returns delivery or an inbound delivery, the **Post Goods Issue** button changes to **Post Goods Receipt.**

Once the delivery document has been posted, the system will generate the new delivery number.

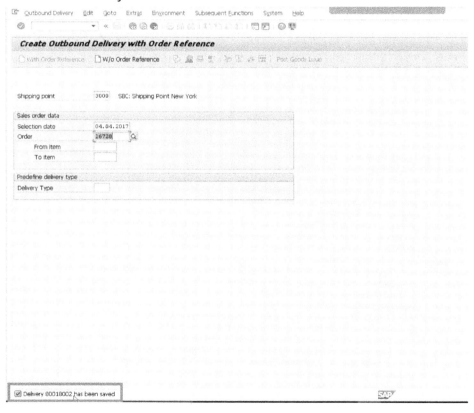

You will be able to display the document flow and review the materials management to verify the inventory posting (See section 7.1.4 - Display a Delivery Document).

Functionality – Create a New Delivery Document (Collective)

The previous step is good for processing individual delivery documents.

However, if you have a large quantity of documents to process, you can use the "collective delivery" transaction.

This functionality will allow you to automatically create all the deliveries for a particular due date in a single step.

To create new delivery documents in a collective way, you have several options:

- Transaction VL10A – List of sales order (at header level) to create the delivery documents
- Transaction VL10C – List of sales orders (at item level) to create the delivery documents
- Transaction VL10E – List of sales orders (at schedule line level) to create the delivery documents
- Transaction VL10G – List of sales orders and purchase orders to create the delivery documents

Note: The functionality to create outbound delivery documents for purchase orders is related to stock transport orders.

To start with, you will access the transaction corresponding to the type of collective delivery you are planning to make. This example will cover in detail the option for sales orders at item level (assuming you want to see the details of the items being shipped).

The corresponding transaction for this is VL10C (sales order items). In this transaction, you will need to enter:

- Shipping point: This is the point where the goods will be delivered from. For some customers, there can be several shipping points for a single plant.

Example: Rush orders dock, regular shipping.

- Delivery creation date: This is the date when the delivery is planned to be executed.
    - By default, the dates appearing here will be configured to follow a specific pattern.

Example: Today's date + 30 days.

Note: Deliveries in the past of the initial delivery date will still appear automatically, as they were supposed to be shipped prior to that date.

- Additional data:
    - You can include additional information regarding the general data (customer, division, etc.), sales order (sales order #, sales office, etc.), materials, and partners.

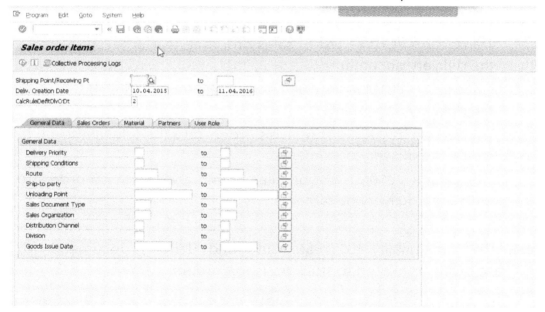

- ❖ After entering this information, select the 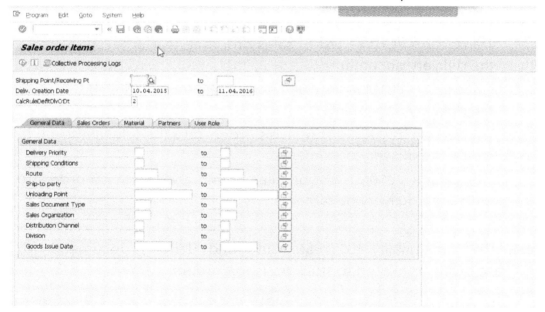 icon or click F8 to get the results.

This screen, which shows all the line items that have a pending item to be delivered, will show for every sales order.

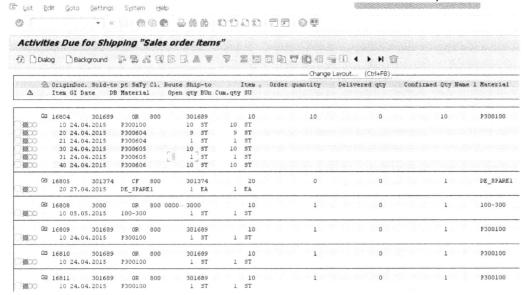

You can select all the items at once with the  icon or select a particular number of icons one at the time. It is also possible to summarize some elements (like weight), and add/hide some of the columns shown via the Change Layout icon.

Please note that if you select several orders, they can only be combined if they have the same header information (shipping point, ship-to). Otherwise, they will be split.

❖ In this case, select an order to convert it to delivery, and only two of the three requested items for delivery (assume the other item was not available for delivery and the delivered items were needed as soon as possible).

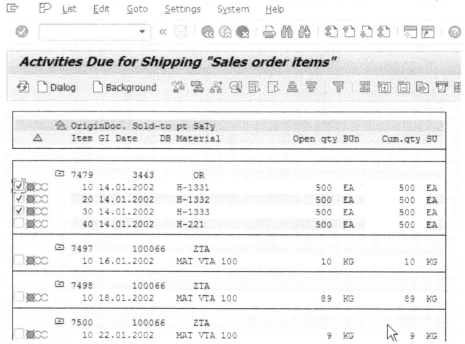

8.1.1.1. Dialog Option

We will select the dialog option, as we want to process only this particular delivery. If we wanted to select several and process them at the same time, we can mark them for background generation.

The dialog will take us to the same screen as if we had used "VA01 – Create delivery", and the user must have access to both transactions to be able to complete the process.

This is the generated screen for the items, and the process to follow is as discussed in the Create a Delivery Document (Individually) section.

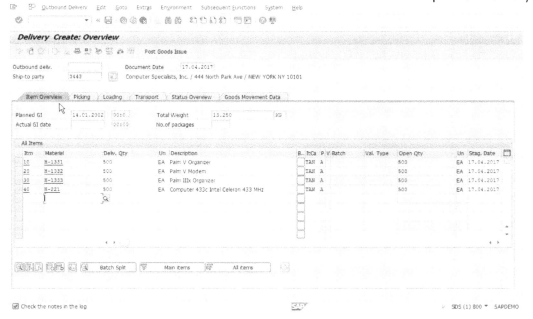

8.1.1.2. Background

In the option for creating a delivery document in the background, select one or more elements to be generated (items) and execute the report.

After this, a list of documents will be generated according to the requirements from the sales order.

The new deliveries are created automatically and, at the end, the system will generate a list of the newly created documents.

If you select several items or lines, and they belong to the same customer, sales organization, shipping point, etc., the system will automatically combine those orders into one delivery.

The reason for this is that the system assumes you want to ship goods in the most efficient way, and unless it has been determined otherwise (via master data or configuration), it will try to minimize the number of different deliveries as much as possible.

On the following screen, two different sales orders (Order 15994 and order 15990) have been selected, both belonging to the same customer

301555. As a result, the system is expected to ship the product in a single delivery order.

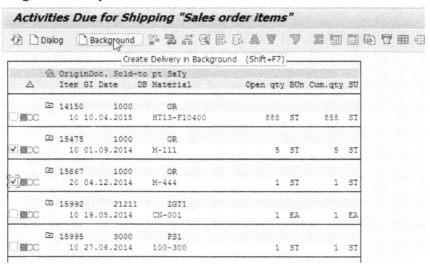

At the end, a list of documents will be generated. After that, the process continues as a normally manual delivery.

Functionality – Modify a Delivery Document

Displaying an Existing Delivery Document	
Menu Path	Logistics > Sales and Distribution > Shipping and Transportation > Outbound Delivery > Modify
Transaction	VL02N

❖ To update an existing delivery document, use transaction VL02N. For this transaction, enter the delivery document number and select the enter icon.

Once the delivery has been saved and the goods issue has been posted, there are very few fields that can be changed. If there are changes required, you need to first reverse the post goods issue (see Section 7.1.5 Canceling Goods Issue).

❖ For the available modifiable fields, enter the changes and save the document.

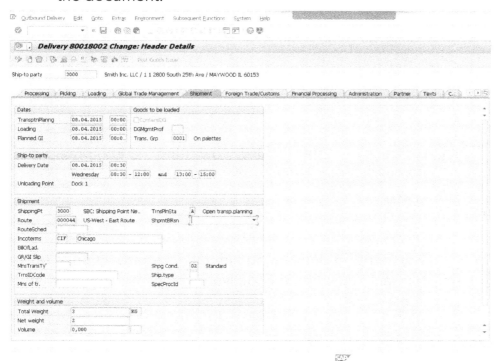

Once you save the document, it will record the changes, displaying a message indicating that the document has been saved.

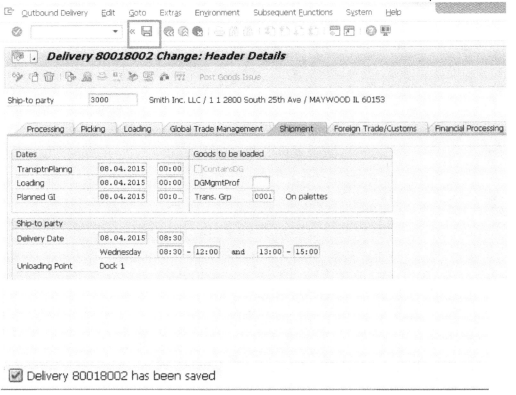

Delivery 80018002 has been saved

Functionality – Display a Delivery Document

Displaying an Existing Delivery Document	
Menu Path	Logistics > Sales and Distribution > Shipping and Transportation > Outbound Delivery > Display
Transaction	VL03N

❖ To display an existing delivery document, use transaction VL03N. For this transaction, enter the delivery document number and select the enter icon.

After this, you will be able to see all the data captured in the delivery. You can also navigate to the materials management movement, and the corresponding accounting posting, by clicking on the document flow icon   .

This will show the different documents posted as a result of the goods issue and the picking.

Once you have done the picking request, an automatic picking request and a materials management document are saved.

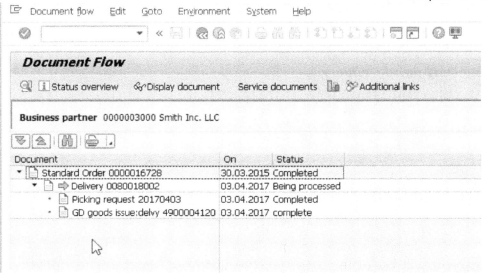

Within the material management document, you can see the posted movement, as well as the accounting document.

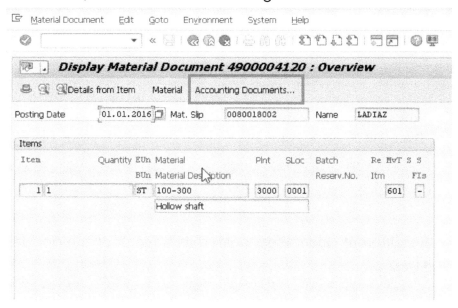

This will show the different accounting documents registered.

If you double-click on the accounting document, you will see the posting.

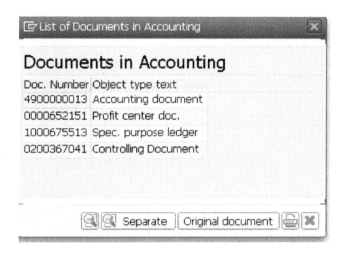

Canceling Goods Issue

In case you need to modify a delivery document that has been already posted, you will need to cancel the goods issue. This process will return the stock to inventory, as well as financially update the corresponding accounts for this movement (like inventory or cost of goods sold financial accounts).

The transaction for this operation is VL09. Here, you will need to enter the parameters to get the list of the deliveries that can be reversed.

Note: If an invoice has been processed, its goods issue cannot be reversed until the corresponding invoice is cancelled.

❖ For this report, after the parameters are entered, select the execute icon to continue.

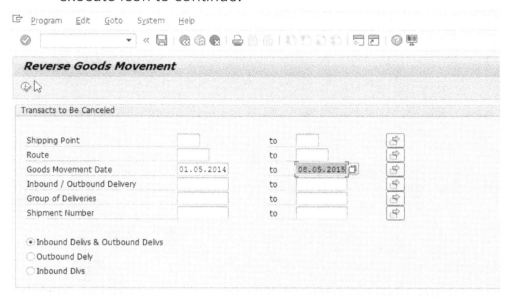

❖ On the following screen, select the delivery you want to reverse and select the execute icon.

Note: The reversal date is always proposed as the date when the transaction is executed. In case you need a different date, prior to executing the reverse process, you will need to set the new date.

Example: Assume you want to reverse the posting to apply on the previous period, but today is May 8. You will need to change the date to April 30 by clicking on **Define Date** and determining the new date.

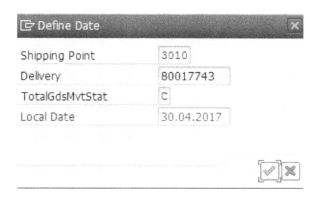

❖ After this, you can post the reverse of the document. The system will raise a confirmation box to ask if you want to continue with the process. Click on the green checkmark to continue.

The system will then indicate that the movement has been correctly posted (or an error message if there was any problem).

8.2. CONFIGURATION

Configuration – New Document Type

Creating a New Document Type	
Menu Path	SPRO > Logistics Execution > Shipping > Deliveries
Transaction	OVLK

The delivery type provides a way to group the different delivery options for the organization.

SAP normally provides the most common delivery types to use.

Examples:

- BV – Cash Sale
- LF – Normal Delivery
- LR – Returns Delivery
- NL – Replenishment Delivery
- NLCC – Replenishment Cross Company.

However, if you need to add a new delivery type, the usual recommendation is to create a new delivery type to fit your needs.

In this example, you will create a new delivery type, copying from LF – Normal Delivery.

❖ First, select the original delivery type (LF) and then select the copy icon.

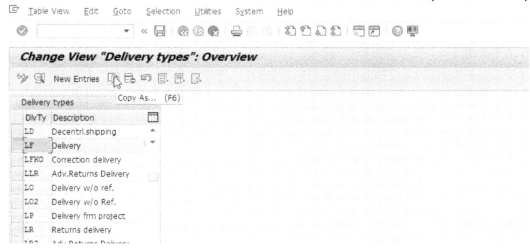

❖ Next, fill out the correct information (according to your needs).

Depending on the parameters included, the delivery will behave in a different way, so it is important to clarify the functionality associated to each field:

Important fields are detailed in the table below:

Field	Use
Delivery Type	ID of the new delivery/description. **Note**: Since you are creating a new document, it is recommended to use "Z" or "Y" at the beginning of the ID (up to four alphanumeric characters) – ZNOR (For Normal)
Document Category	Type of operation for logistics. Leave "J" for outbound delivery.
NR in Assgt	Number range internally assigned which will be the number range for the documents. The system will assign automatically the next available number within the specified range
No. Range Ext	Number range externally assigned. The user creating the delivery document must assign the delivery number. This is used commonly when an external system creates the delivery number and that delivery is interfaced with SAP. Then, you can maintain the same number across both systems.
Item No Increment	The counter by which the item numbers are created. **Example**: If the standard is left as it is, then the item number will be: 10, 20, 30, etc.
Order Required	If the delivery can be created based on a sales order or other type of document (purchase order, project, etc.)
Default Ord. Type	Default order type for deliveries without a reference document.
Item Requirement	Item requirement for item delivery created without a reference document. **Note**: A requirement is a condition that needs to be fulfilled for the item to be included in the delivery.
Delivery Split – WhNo	Delivery split according to warehouse number. If the items have different warehouse numbers and the checkmark has been included, two or more different delivery numbers will be generated, separating the items by the warehouse number.

Field	Use
Delivery Split Part	Delivery split according to different partner. If different partners are included on the delivery, then the deliveries will be split according those partners.
Rescheduling	Indicates if the delivery can be re-scheduled or if it must be delivered on the original scheduled date.
Automatic Packing	Indicates if the system will try to find the automatic packing instructions.
Distribution Mode	Indicates how the delivery must be distributed to the Warehouse Management System.
Gen Pack Matl Item	Indicates if the delivery must generate items automatically for handling units packaging materials.
Screen Seq Group	The sequence of the different fields to be shown on the screen.
Display Range	The scope of display that will be shown by default in the delivery creation. **Note**: The user can change the scope during creation.

Configuration – Copy Control

Copy Control	
Menu Path	SPRO> Logistics Execution > Shipping > Copying Control > Specify Copy Control for Deliveries
Transaction	VTLA

In the copy control, you establish the relationship between a sales order and a delivery. Data is copied automatically to the delivery that can be configured on this transaction.

You will need to include all possible combinations that you will allow for your document types. If a particular combination between sales orders and deliveries is not entered, then you won't be able to create a delivery document based on that particular document type.

This is useful for when you have users that can create only certain types of deliveries, e.g.: rush orders, special orders, etc., so only those can be created from the specified sales orders.

There are elements that can be configured at header level, like delivery split, while others are included at item level.

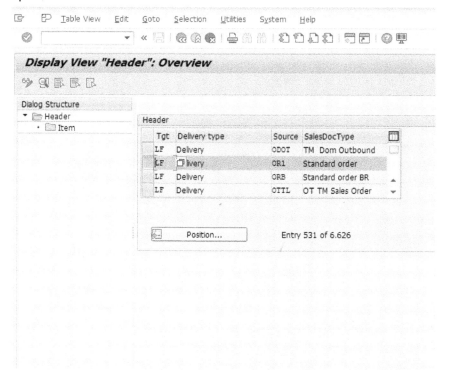

You can configure the copy control at Header level or item level.

❖ To access the configuration at Header level, select the combination of documents you need, and select the "details" option.

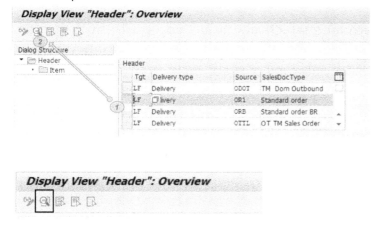

At header level, there are different important fields

- Order requirements include which conditions must be in place for the order to be copied to the delivery. If those conditions are not met, the source document will not be copied to the delivery. In case you need particular checks before your document is copied, there are available standard validations and you can define your own (via ABAP).

- Combination requirements determine if different orders can be combined in one delivery or not. This is useful when you are shipping several sales order for a particular customer (to minimize shipping costs) or if you have a delivery route when you are shipping to several customers in a single shipment along a route.

- Header data determines which fields are copied from the sales order to the delivery. By default, in the standard formula 001 the most commonly used data are copied, including plant, material, and quantity.

- If you need to copy additional data, the standard formulas can be updated via ABAP.

❖ To view the copy control at item level, select the combination and double-click on the "Item" folder.

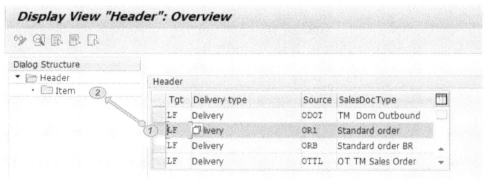

At item level, you will have the detailed copy control from sales order item to delivery item.

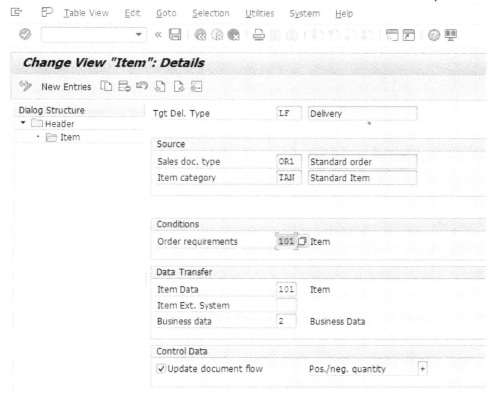

You can also define requirements for an item to be copied or not to a delivery.

Example: you might not want to have a "Free goods" item on a particular delivery type.

Also, you can define the fields that are to be copied at item level from the sales order to the delivery.

"Update document flow" is relevant if you want the copied data to be part of the original document flow. You might not want to be on the document flow if the original document only serves as a reference document, but you don't want the delivery to be linked to it.

The positive, negative, or zero effect on quantity refers to how the quantity copied will affect the quantity pending to be completed on the source document.

Example: In a sales order for 100 pieces, if you copy 80, the referenced quantity increases (positive effect) and you only have 20 pieces left to deliver.

A zero effect will be a document that you use as a template and don't need to track the quantity referenced in it.

Configuration – Item Categories

Delivery Item Category	
Menu Path	SPRO > Logistics Execution > Shipping > Deliveries > Define Item Categories for Deliveries
Transaction	OVLP

The item categories in the delivery determine the behavior for each one of the delivery items.

It is possible for the same deliveries to have different item categories, each with their own pre-requisites and defaults.

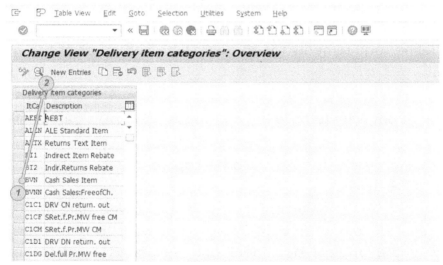

To create a new item category, use the "New entries" button or copy an existing one (recommended).

The most commonly used item categories are:

- TAN – Standard Item
- TATX – Text item

- TANN – Free of charge item
- TAX – Non stock item
- REN – Returns item
- NL – Stock Transport order
- NLCC – Intercompany sales

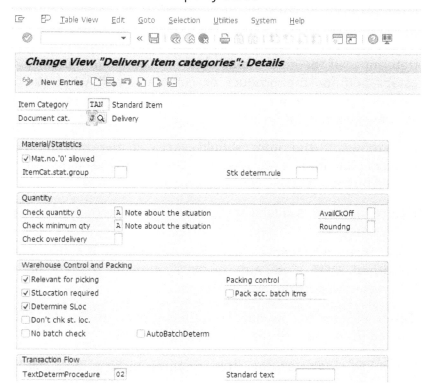

In this detail, configure if the item is relevant for picking, if it requires and storage location, etc.

Automatic checks can be turned on or off depending on your requirements.

Example: You might not want to do an availability check when carrying out a particular delivery (checking if there is enough inventory to fulfil your order), so mark the corresponding indicator.

There are several important fields in this section, as indicated in the following table:

Field	Use
Mat No "0" allowed	If marked, indicates that a material with a 0 quantity is allowed in the delivery. **Example**: A retail item can be left with a 0 quantity.
Check quantity 0	Review if the quantity in the delivery has been left as 0, and if it has, determine if a no message, a warning (note about the situation), or an error should be issued.
Check minimum quantity	Determines if the item should check the minimum quantity established for the product or customer, and what the behavior should be if this minimum quantity is not met (no message, warning or error).
Check over delivery	Determines if the item should check if the maximum delivery quantity is surpassed, and what the behavior should be (no message, warning, error).
AvalCkOff	Determines if no availability check should be carried out for this item. **Note**: This is a "negative" logic. You can indicate if it should be turned "OFF". If you indicate "YES", it means that you do NOT desire to perform availability check.
Rounding	Determines for this item if the rounding quantity should be applied (if the material has a rounding quantity).
Relevant for Picking	If marked, indicates the item requires picking, and this information must be filled out in the delivery before continuing.
StLoc Required	If marked, indicates the item must have the storage location registered before continuing.
Determine SLoc	If marked, indicates the storage location must be determined automatically. **Note**: If you are going to mark this indicator, you must also configure the parameters, which will allow determining the storage location.
Do not check St Loc	If marked, indicates the item should not check if the material is created on the particular storage location where it will be delivered from.
No batch check	If marked, indicates the item should not check for the existence of the batch number registered on the delivery.

Field	Use
AutoBatchDeterm	If marked, indicates the item should perform automatic batch determination. **Note**: If you mark this indicator, you must also configure the parameters to automatically determine the batch.
Packing control	If marked, indicates you will activate the packing control to the item, and if the item can be packed or MUST be packed. **Note**: If marked, all the packing relevant information like packaging instructions, = and the relevant configuration should be also completed.
Pack Acc Batch items	If marked, the item and each one of its batches must be packed before completing the delivery. Otherwise, only the main item can be packed.

Configuration – Item Category Determination

Define Item Categories for Deliveries	
Menu Path	SPRO > Logistics Execution > Shipping > Deliveries > Define Item Category Determination in Deliveries
Transaction	0184

In this transaction, link between the delivery type and the item category will be made.

The combination of delivery type, item category group, usage, and item category for higher-level item determines the item category to be used.

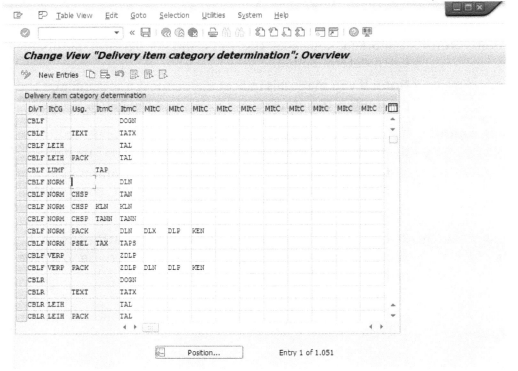

The delivery type needs to determine at least one item category to operate correctly.

The item category group is associated to the material master at sales area level.

The usage is how the item will be used in the transaction. The most common uses are: "Blank" or NORM (the standard use for shipping stock). Other uses are specific like PACK for shipping additional packaging; FREE for free goods, CHSP for batch split, etc.

Note: The complete list of item usages can be found on SPRO> Logistics Execution> Shipping > Deliveries > Define Item Category Usage.

The higher-level item category group is where you have a sub-item that depends on another item, and then the sub-item item category will depend on its parent item to determine the correct one.

With these four different fields, you will be able to determine the appropriate item category group to be used as a default.

You might want to include additional manual item categories that will be allowed. This data will be available to be manually updated when the user is executing the delivery

If no alternative item category is included, only the default item category will be determined, and the user won't have the option to change it.

Configuration – Number Ranges for Deliveries

Number Ranges for Deliveries	
Menu Path	SPRO > Logistics Execution > Shipping > Deliveries > Define Number Ranges for Deliveries
Transaction	VN01

In this transaction, you will define the available number ranges for the delivery types.

IMPORTANT: The number ranges interval is shared between sales orders, deliveries, and billing documents.

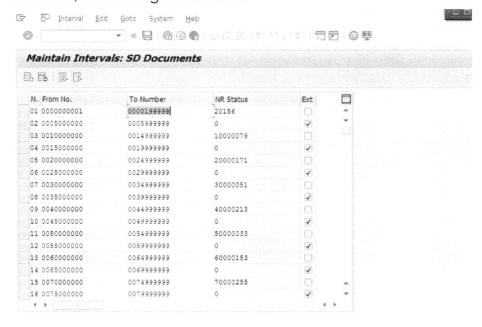

Each delivery document created is identified on the system with a unique ID number.

There are two types of number ranges: internally assigned by the system and externally assigned. The most commonly used is the internal option, where the system keeps track of the consecutive numbers, and with each new delivery document created, the interval is automatically updated. The externally assigned number is normally used if you are using an interface where you want to maintain the same reference number in both systems. Another reason to use an externally assigned number is if there are any business or legal requirements to identify the deliveries.

All of the original documents from SAP are normally already assigned to an existing interval.

It is common practice to separate groups of delivery types in different intervals, as this will tell you just by looking at the number of the document whether it is a sales delivery, a return, or a stock transfer.

IMPORTANT: The number ranges are non-transportable, which means you will have to re-create them in each environment. In a new implementation project, this will be part of the "manual" activities on the cutover plan. For an already productive environment, the system will have to be open for customizing for the time you are doing the changes.

❖ Select the "Edit intervals" option. In there, you can edit an existing range, specifying from which number to which number the range will cover. For internally assigned ranges, there is a column called "NR Status - Number range status," which tells you the most up-to-date document number within that range.

The "To-Number" cannot be lower than the "NR Status number" for automatically assigned ranges.

The option "Ext" indicates if the range will be internal or external. If it is external, meaning you will need to manually indicate the document number, then click the check box to ON. Otherwise, you need to leave it OFF.

It is not recommended to create intervals too granular, as this will reduce the available numbers you will have for each interval, especially if you are implementing in a company with a high transaction volume. By doing this, you run the risk of running out of available numbers in an interval and needing to create a new interval, assign it to the documents, etc.

9. BILLING

9.1. USES AND FUNCTIONALITY

Once the sales order and the delivery process have been completed (with the goods issue), it is now possible to create an invoice for these documents. When you generate an invoice to the customer, several things happen automatically in the system:

- An accounting document is generated, where normally the customer account is charged, and the revenue account is increased.
- In AR, the financial document generates an open receivable with the customer, which will only be closed when the payment is received.
- The sales order is marked as completely billed.
- The delivery document is also marked as completely billed.

Note: Some documents will not require a delivery process (like credit and debit memos), and can be invoiced right away from the sales order.

The following examples will cover the process of generating the invoice after the delivery. The process to create an invoice from a sales order is similar, but the origin document to the invoice will be the sales order instead of the delivery.

Functionality – Create a New Invoice (Individually)

Creating a New Invoice – Individually	
Menu Path	Logistics > Sales and Distribution > Billing > Billing Document > Create
Transaction	VF01

As with the document types, the invoices are composed of header and items.

For an individual document, you can enter it in the following three ways:

- With reference to a sales order
- With reference to a delivery
- Without reference.

When creating a new invoice, you will also need to enter at least the invoice type to be generated.

Note: If you leave this field blank, the system will generate the default invoice type for the reference document. If none has been configured, this field must be entered manually.

For the different dates that are available, you can enter a specific date when you want the invoice to calculate the pricing or to be set as a billing date.

Note: If you leave these fields blank, the system will take the current date to post the document.

In the following example, the services entered were rendered the same as the pricing date. However, imagine that the next 30 days were negotiated to start from the end of the month.

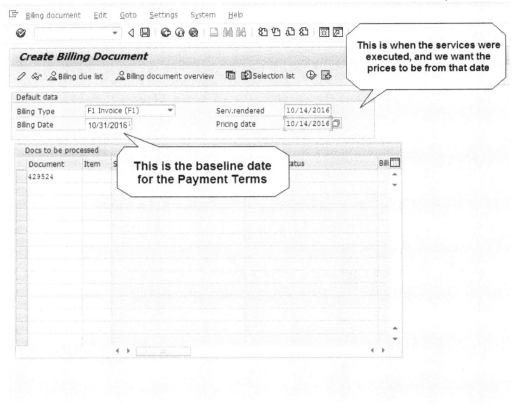

❖ On this screen, select the enter icon and proceed to the next screen. Then verify that all data is correct and save the document. If you have several documents to invoice, you can also enter a list of the documents here.

Note: In case there is any error on the invoice, it is a better option to cancel the invoice generation by selecting the cancel icon and correcting the preceding documents.

The accounting documents have a different number range than invoices. Sometimes, the users ask to homologate the two number ranges: the invoice and the financial document, and even the "pre-printed" or consecutive for printed (or electronic invoices). By definition and standard configuration, they are independent and this is SAP recommendation as a best practice. If this is a mandatory requirement, it must be done by a combination of configuration and ABAP developments.

Once you have saved the document, you will get the invoice number.

☑ Document 90746677 has been saved

Also, if you go back to display or update the invoice, you can see the accounting documents generated for this invoice and the corresponding postings.

❖ To see the detail of the amounts and accounts posted, select the display document icon.

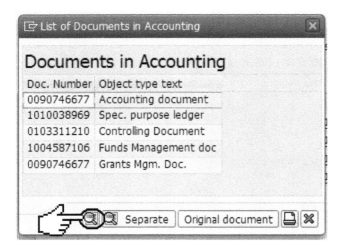

Functionality – Invoice Split

Creating a New Invoice – Invoice Split	
Menu Path	Logistics > Sales and Distribution > Billing > Billing Document > Create
Transaction	VF01

In a document list, if the invoices being created share the billing date, customer, and other common characteristics, the system will create one consolidated invoice with all the items on the same invoice. In some cases, the criteria to merge the invoice will not be met, so the system will generate several invoices. This is known as an invoice split. There are already some predefined routines that can be used to influence the criteria for the invoice split. This will be discussed in more detail in the configuration section for the copy control of invoices.

In case these routines do not fit your company, they can be adapted via ABAP.

❖ This is how the screen will look if the invoice is split. If you need further detail on why the invoice was split, select the **Split analysis** button, where you need to select two invoices to determine what the criteria was to split them.

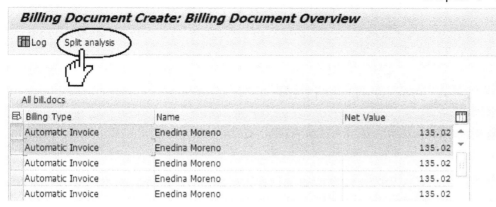

The system will explain why the invoices were split. The information in columns 0001, 0002 is the detail on the data that was different.

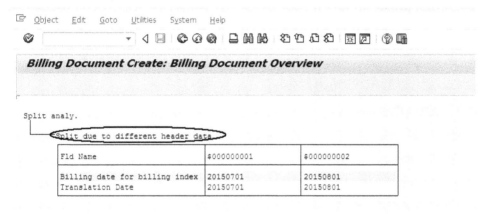

From here, you just need to go back to the original split screen and save the documents, and the system will generate the corresponding invoices.

Note: Upon saving, you will only get the last number of all the invoices generated, but you can still identify the invoices created from your original documents list using the document flow functionality.

Functionality – Create a New Invoice (Collective)

Creating a New Invoice – Collective	
Menu Path	Logistics > Sales and Distribution > Billing > Billing Document > Process Billing Due List
Transaction	VF04

In case you have a large number of invoices, you can use the collective billing to have the working list of documents and process them collectively.

❖ On the selection screen, enter the parameters to filter the desired list of documents to be invoiced. If you leave all parameters blank, the system will propose all the documents that will have a billing date within the desired period.

❖ In the tab for default data, enter data that will apply as a default for all the invoices generated collectively. In the tab for batch and update, enter information to be used for a batch processing of the invoices.

❖ Once you have the parameters ready, you can select the **Display Bill List** button ⊕ DisplayBillList , and a list of all documents pending to be invoiced will be created.

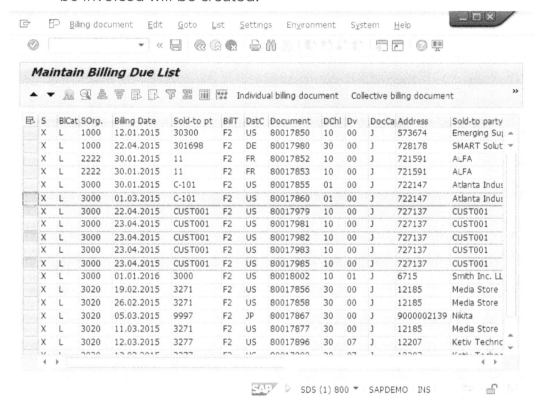

Once you have the selected list, you can choose to process them:

- Individually
- Collectively (on background)
  - o In case some invoice can be merged, the system will merge them, otherwise they will be split.
- Collectively (on line)

9.1.1.1. Individual Billing Document

This option will be similar to processing the invoice (or invoice list) on the individual transaction VF01. For this detail, please refer to Section 8.1.1 Functionality – Create a New Invoice (Individually)

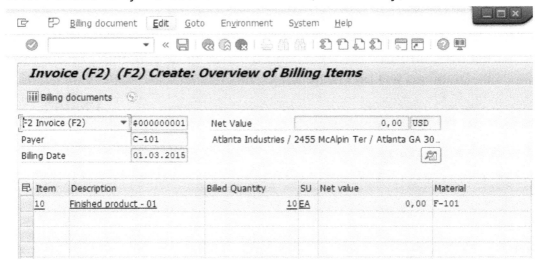

9.1.1.2. Collective Billing Document (Background)

In this option, the system processes the invoice on the background, so it will not display any transaction or confirmation screen until it is finished.

❖ Once the process is finished, you can see the collective run log by selecting the log button ▦ . This log will give us the count of generated documents, as well as the number of errors.

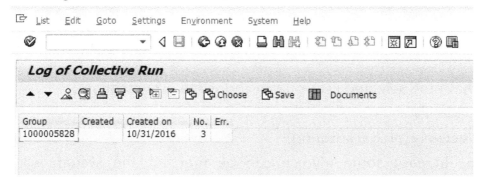

❖ In case you need to see the list of documents, select the **Documents** button, and you can see the invoice document number on the Document column.

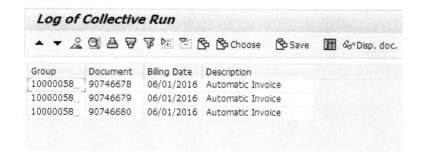

❖ From here, select a row and use the **Disp. doc.** button to see the generated invoice, or you can go back to the original screen.

In the billing due list, you will see the processed invoices with an updated status on the rightmost columns of the report. Those invoices that were not processed because of an error, or where the process was cancelled, are marked with an "X". Those invoices processed correctly will show a green check mark. And in addition to this, if they were processed on background, the ID for the collective run will be shown.

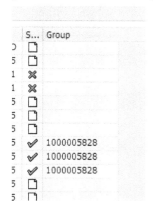

Functionality – Modify an Existing Invoice

Modifying an Existing Invoice	
Menu Path	Logistics > Sales and Distribution > Billing > Billing Document > Change
Transaction	VF02

You can modify an existing invoice using transaction VF02.

❖ To update it, enter the invoice document number and click enter.

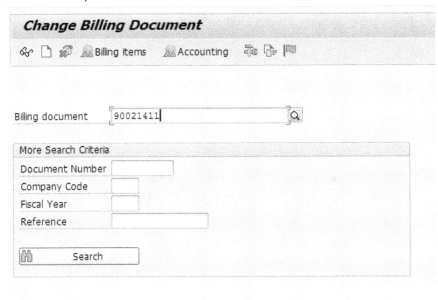

Change Billing Document

⚒ ☐ 🖋 ⚒ Billing items   ⚒ Accounting   🖨 🖨 🏳

Billing document   90021411   🔍

More Search Criteria	
Document Number	
Company Code	
Fiscal Year	
Reference	

🔍   Search

Once the invoice has been created, only a few fields can be edited (marked in yellow). If you want to edit an unavailable field, you will need to cancel the invoice.

🖼 ▾   **Invoice 90746663 (   ) Change : Header data**

🖨 ⚒ Billing items   ⚒ Accounting   🖼 Output

In... ▾ 90746663
Payer   100101
Created by   Created on   10/24/2016 Time   09:51:02

| Header | Head.prtnrs | Conditions | ForTrade/Customs | Head.text |

Accounting Data

Billing Date	10/01/2016	Document Currency	USD
Company Code		☐ Set exchange rt	
Reference	0090746663	Exchange rate-accntg	1.00000
Assignment		Payment Method	
Trading Partner		Dunning Area	24 Finance Alcohol
Fixed value date		Dunning key	
Addlt.value days	0	Dunning block	Freed for dunning
AcctAssgGr	01 Domestic Revenues		
Posting Status	Error in Accounting Interface		

Price data

Price List		Exch. Rate Type	
Customer group		Agreement	
Price group			
Terms of Paymen	0001	Pay immediately w/o deduction	
Incoterms	FOB	ORIGINATION	
Pricing procedure			

Taxes

Destination Country	US	Region	TX
TaxClass1-Cust.	1 0 0 1	County code	
VAT Registration No.		City code	
Country sls.tax no.	US	Export	
Origin sls.tax no.	A	Ship-to party	☐ EU triangular deal

General information

Sales Organization		Inv.list type	LR
Distribution Channel	01	Billing date	
Division	07	Cancld bil.dc	
Sales district		☐ Cancelled	

Functionality – Display an Existing Invoice

Modifying an Existing Invoice	
Menu Path	Logistics > Sales and Distribution > Billing > Billing Document > Display
Transaction	VF03

You can display an existing invoice using transaction VF03.

❖ First, enter the invoice number, and click enter or select the green checkmark button to continue.

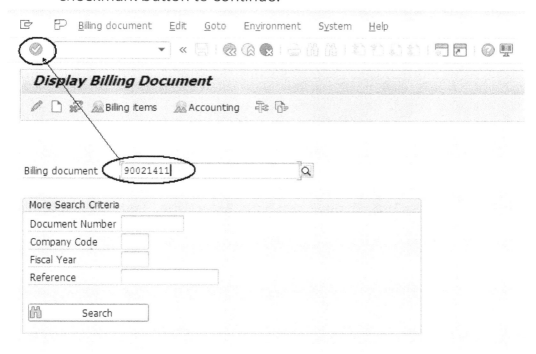

From here, you will see the details of the invoice and all the data included on it.

Note: In this transaction you won't be able to modify any field

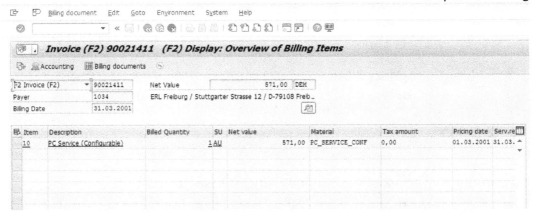

9.1.1.3. Displaying the Account Determination

In some cases, especially at the beginning of a project, you might want to know how the revenue accounts were determined (due to incorrect postings or corrections needed).

Once the invoice is posted, you can display the account determination as follows.

❖ From the menu, select Environment > Acc.determ.analysis > and select the desired account type.

Example: To review the revenue account, select the Revenue accounts option.

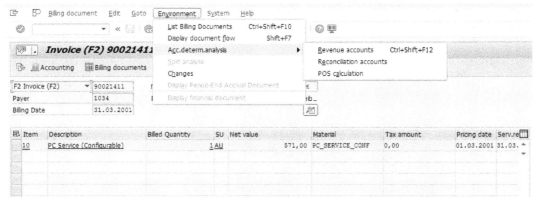

This will tell you the information used to determine a particular account.

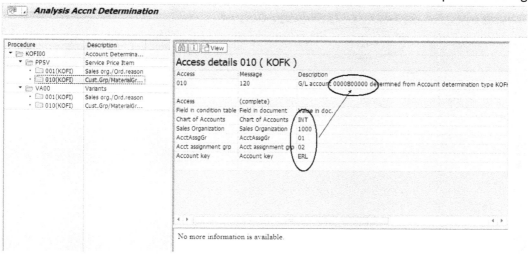

9.1.1.4. Reviewing the Output Log (Printing the Invoice Form)

In some cases, you need to review the output log of the invoice, like to solve a printing issue, and determine if the invoice has already been printed or not.

Once you are in the display (or update) section of the invoice, you can see the log of the printing document.

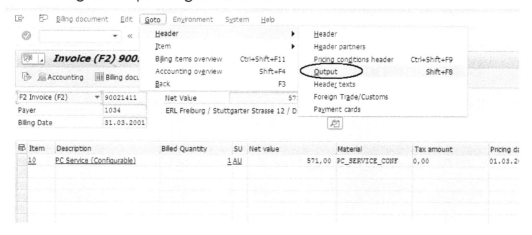

From here, you can select the appropriate message (there might be more than one), and view the printing log.

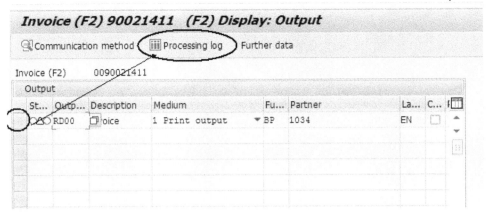

This will give you a log of the printout. If there were any errors, it will indicate it on the log, and you will be able to see what the problem was.

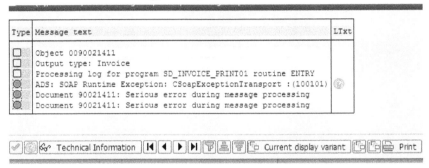

9.2. CONFIGURATION

Configuration – New Document Type

Creating a New Document Type	
Menu Path	SPRO > SD > Billing > Billing Documents > Define Billing Types > Define Billing Types
Transaction	SPRO

The Standard R/3 system provides a list of commonly used invoices, being the most frequently used:

- F2 – Invoice
- G2 – Credit memo
- L2 – Debit memo

In case you need to define your own invoice, you can use the standard as a reference and modify according to your needs.

The procedure to create a new invoice document type is as follows:

❖ Select a document to make reference to, select the copy icon, select the enter icon, and enter the new invoice type and its description.

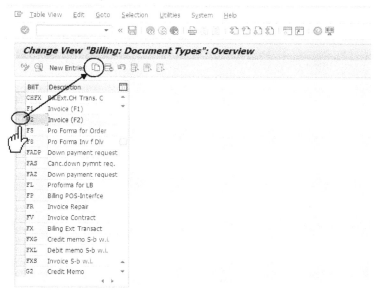

If you are copying the invoice, you will get the following message:

❖ Select Yes.

This will copy all the information, including the references of copy control from other documents to the invoice (either sales orders or delivery documents).

❖ Once you have created the new entry, modify its parameters according to what you need.

In the following table, you will find the most relevant parameters commonly used to adapt an invoice:

Field	Use
Number Range	Number range to be associated to the invoice document type. **Note**: In some cases, different number ranges are created depending on the invoice type to make it easier to identify in reports, developments, etc.
SD Doc Category	Indicates type of operation: M – Invoice N – Invoice cancellation O – Credit memo P – Debit memo
Document Type	Finance document type to be used in conjunction with the invoice.
Cancellation Billing Type	Type of invoice to be posted automatically whenever a cancellation of an invoice is created. **Note**: A cancellation of an invoice in SAP does not delete the original invoice. The system marks the original one as cancelled and it posts a new cancellation invoice with the reverse postings to finance.
Account Determination Procedure	Here you can assign the procedure to be used for the account determination.
Doc Pricing Procedure	Assigning the corresponding pricing procedure so you can calculate prices for the invoice.
Output Determination Procedure	This allows to determine the output (form) to be printed out from the invoice. The assigned output type mentioned here is the default output to be used for the invoice.

Configuration – Copy Control

Creating a New Document Type	
Menu Path	SPRO > SD > Billing > Billing Documents > Maintain Copying Control for Billing Documents
Transaction	SPRO

The copy control from billing determines which documents can be copied as a source to the invoice, and from them, which fields will be transferred.

It also allows you to enter validations before the items are copied and requirements to avoid copying items that do not fill our organization criteria.

Example: Let's assume your company has a requirement for a billing type, which only can invoice documents, which are delivery-related (as opposed to sales order related).

In this case, you will configure in the "requirements", one of the routines that validates the mentioned business need.

Depending on the type of invoice you are doing and the reference document being referenced, you will choose:

- Sales document to billing documents (e.g.: credit memos, debit memos, sales with no deliveries)
- Billing document to billing documents (e.g.: invoice cancellation)
- Delivery document to billing documents (e.g.: sales with deliveries)

The procedures for the different options are fairly similar. This example will include the option to reference for copy control between delivery documents to billing document.

On the left side of the screen are the folders for header/item. On the right is the list of documents being copied to and from (in those columns, there is first the destination and then the source).

❖ Select the combination you want to update, if it is a standard combination.

In the case that you have created new document types and you did not copy them from the standard, or mentioned they were not relevant for copy control, you will need to create (or copy) the corresponding combinations here.

To configure the details of the copy control at header level, you will need to select the desired combination and click on the details button. There are a certain number of parameters that can be updated and that will influence the behavior of the new invoice upon creation.

This is the detail at header level:

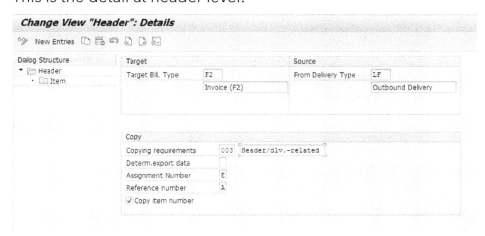

The copy control routines are only used when creating a new invoice that is being copied from a previous document.

Once an invoice is created, any routine or validation included in the configuration will not be executed again.

Field	Use
Copying Requirements	This is an ABAP routine to determine if the source document (delivery or invoice) can be copied to the invoice. If the requirements are not met, the invoice will not be generated. SAP provides standard routines, but you can create new routines in transaction VOFM > Copying Requirements > Billing Documents
Determine Export Data	Defines if export data is re-determined at invoice time or is copied from the delivery/sales document.
Assignment Number	This information will be copied to the financial document. Depending on the parameter, it will be the information stored in the assignment field.
Reference Number	This information will be copied to the financial document. Depending on the parameter, it will be the information stored in the reference field. 1. A: Customer purchase order 2. B: Sales order number 3. C: Delivery number 4. D: External delivery number 5. E: Actual invoice number
Copy Item Number	If the invoice will copy the item number from the original document. **Note**: If you are copying partially from the source or merging two different documents into one (example, several deliveries in one invoice), then this parameter is not met.

At item level, there are several parameters that are also very important for influencing the functionality; for example, if re-pricing is done, or if an invoice will be kept together or split between several items.

For each of the different item categories within a document type, there are different rules for influencing the functionality. The main parameters to do this are:

Field	Use
Copying Requirements	Similar to the header level, but at item level, indicates f information from the item doesn't fulfill certain parameters, the item will not be copied into the new document
Data VBRK/VBRP	This parameter can determine an invoice split. Please choose carefully from the options provided (or if creating a new one), given that it could split the source document (e.g. a delivery document) into several invoices (instead of one), depending on the data. **Note**: This might be a desired outcome, but most often the invoices should be kept as consolidated as possible.
Billing Quantity	This indicates the quantity that will be copied to the invoice. Normally it is the delivered quantity minus anything already invoiced, but there are exceptions like ProForma invoice, where the quantity is that of the sales order.
Positive/Negative	Depend on if it is a regular invoice, a credit memo, or a debit memo.

Pricing Type	Indicates if the pricing is copied from the sales order or is re-calculated at invoice type. **Note**: If it is re-calculated, be aware that the final invoice might have a different price than the original sales order, and this could cause problems for the customer.

Configuration – Account Determination

As previously mentioned, the account determination process (for revenue, reconciliation, or cash accounts) uses the condition technique.

This section will cover how to create data relevant for your master data and how to assign those new parameters to determine your accounts.

9.2.2.1. Parameters for Master Data

Account Determination for Revenue – Account Assignment Groups	
Menu Path	SPRO > SD> Basic Functions > Account Assignment > Costing > Revenue Account Determination > Check Master Data for Account Assignment
Transaction	SPRO

The account assignment group is optional, but very helpful if you have a complex revenue account determination strategy.

Example: On the one hand, if all your revenues fall into the same account (regardless of the material or customer type), and they are only differentiated by the document type (say local vs. export documents), and then it might not be necessary to create new account assignment groups. On the other hand, if your environment requires a very detailed account assignment or varies by materials, customers, or other concepts, then you will have to break down the account assignment groups according to your needs. The procedure to determine the actual assignment group for the material and the customer is very similar, so only the materials will be explained.

❖ First, select the option you require (Materials: Account Assignment Group [or customers]).

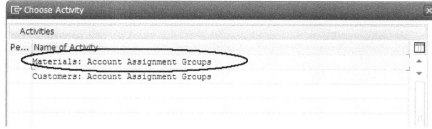

❖ Then select the **New Entries** button, enter the account assignment group ID and its description, and save.

9.2.2.2. Account Determination

Account Determination for Revenue – Account Determination	
Menu Path	SPRO > SD> Basic Functions > Account Assignment > Costing > Revenue Account Determination > Assign G/L Accounts
Transaction	SPRO

Once the account assignment groups have been created in configuration, you can include them on the master data for your materials and customers.

In configuration, you will also include the configuration for the account determination provided by finance.

SAP provides several combinations to determine the accounts. The most commonly used are the "Acct Key" (005) or General (004) options, although you can go as detailed, as you need.

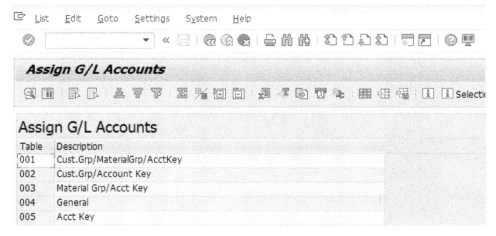

If you have a relatively small number of accounts, you can use the most general assignment, and by exception use the more detailed account keys.

Example: Let's say that 80% of your materials/customers will fall under "General Revenue Account." You can use option 005 for this, and for the exceptions, you can use option 003.

For all of them (or depending on your condition tables), you will normally have:

- Condition type (normally KOFI or KOFK – if you are using CO)
- Chart of accounts
- Sales organization
- Account key
  - The most common ones are:
    - ERL – REVENUE – for regular sales
    - ERS – Sales deductions – for credit memos/discounts
    - ERF – Freight – (in case you need to separate sales from product and freight)
    - MWS – Taxes

All these combinations will determine either:

- Financial account
- Accruals account

Note: This is only used if you configured an "accruals" condition type in your pricing procedure.

Note: For all your operations that will post to accounting, you need to determine at least one financial account.

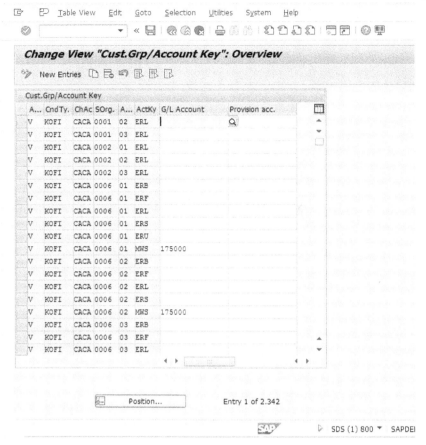

10. PRINTING FORMS

10.1. USES AND FUNCTIONALITY

The most common use for forms printout is on the delivery and billing processes, where printed documents normally need to accompany the goods while in transit (like bill of lading, customs documentation for exports, etc.). Also, in some cases, an invoice is printed out and sent to the customers.

In SAP, these documents can be printed out automatically once the documents are saved, or they can be set to print manually on a process triggered by the user.

Note: In large companies, due to the documents volume, the printout process (or email generation) is a process left to run in background at night.

This chapter will cover in detail how to determine the printers for invoices (being the most used option). The functionality for determining the output for deliveries and sales documents is similar, so deliveries will be covered more briefly.

Functionality – Manually Printing Delivery Documents

Menu Path	SAP Menu > Logistics > Sales and Distribution > Shipping and Transportation > Communication / Printing > Outbound Delivery Output
Transaction	VL71

- ❖ On this screen, to enter the output type and the processing mode.
  - o Normally, for first printing, processing mode = 1
  - o For re-prints, processing mode = 2

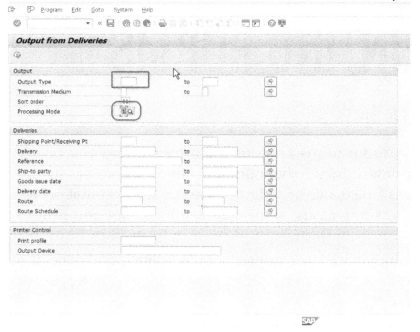

If you have a particular document to print, you can enter it (or a list of documents) in the additional parameters.

❖ Once you have all the required filters, select the execute icon
.

❖ After this, you will get a list of all the available documents matching your criteria. You can select one or all the documents and execute

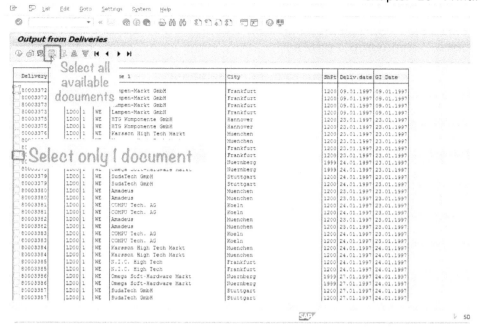

This will print to the default printer configured for the document type. However, you can change the printer on the output print parameters, as they appear to confirm your printout.

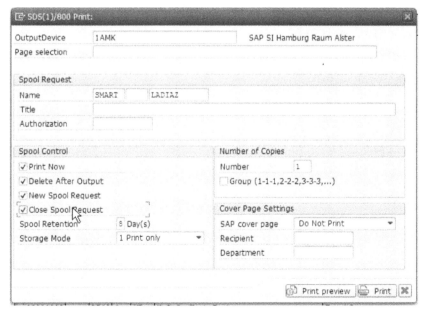

What you will need to define there is:

Field	Use
Output Device	Name of the printer.
Print now	Check if you want to print immediately.
Delete After Output	If you want to release the spool (log) generated for the printout.
New Spool Request	If you want to generate a new spool request **Note:** This is recommended if you want each document to be printed out separately. If you want to consolidate several documents and print as one, then disable this option.
Close Spool Request	If you are closing the spool after printing.
Spool Retention	Number of days a spool will be maintained in the database.
SAP Cover Page	Do not print (recommended).

❖ Then, select {Print Preview} or {Print}, depending on the option desired

For our example, we included an option to preview the document. The following example is the standard form, as it normally appears when SAP is delivered. This need to be adapted for your company needs either by your or the ABAP team.

CCS Industrial
0 0 3300 Main Street
SAN DIEGO CA   92121

Delivery note

Shipping   information

Delivery note number/date	80007251	/ 20.06.2000
Customer's PO number/date	daadsfasdf	
Order number/date	6363	/ 20.06.2000
Customer number	3970	

Conditions		Weight - Volume		
Shipping	Standard	Total weight	580	KG
Delivery	CIF Cost Insurance Freig	Net weight	520	KG
		Total volume	1,560	M3

Conditions		Weight - Volume		
Shipping	Standard	Total weight	580	KG
Delivery	CIF Cost Insurance Freig	Net weight	520	KG
		Total volume	1,560	M3

Shipping   details

Item	Material Description	Quantity		Weight	
000010	P-109	2	ST	580	KG
	Pump cast steel IDESNORM 170-230				

❖ If you want to print preview the document before it gets sent to the printer, you can select one document and press the ⬚ icon.

If you wish to change the parameters for all documents selected, you can do so by choosing the following menu option: Edit > Printer default

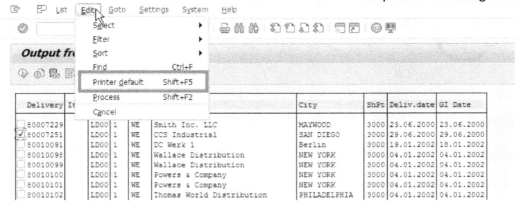

All the parameters previously mentioned will appear here. These parameters will apply for all the documents selected.

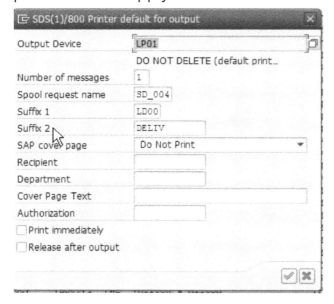

Functionality – Manually Printing Invoices

Creating Output Determination for Invoices	
Menu Path	Sap Menu > Logistics > Sales and Distribution > Billing > Output > Issue Billing Document
Transaction	VF31

10.1.1.1.Standard Formats

SAP provides the standard formats for your use. Normally, it is recommended that you copy the standard document and modify/adapt to your needs. The most commonly used documents for invoices are:

- RD00 – Invoice
- FUCO – Certificate of origin – US
- FUCI – Commercial invoice
- FUEP – Export Packing list
- FUPI – Pro Forma Invoice US

10.1.1.2. Transaction Functionality

First, enter the desired parameters, and if possible, enter the documents pending to print to expedite the process.

Note: If you execute without any parameters, the system will bring all pending invoices to print. If you need to re-print a document already processed, please select option "2 – Repeat processing".

❖ After entering the parameters, select the execute icon.

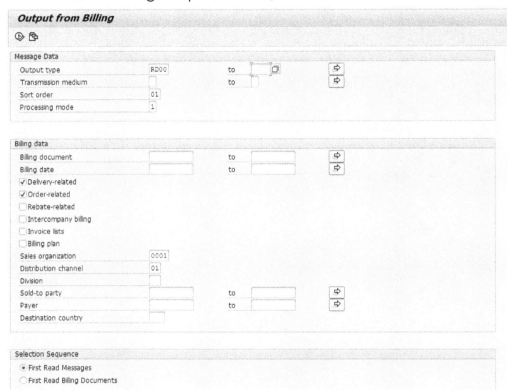

You will get the results list of the documents. There are two options for the documents.

❖ Select them and execute to print out the document (or send it to whatever communication means defined). Select the item and print preview to show a preview of the document.

Output from Billing

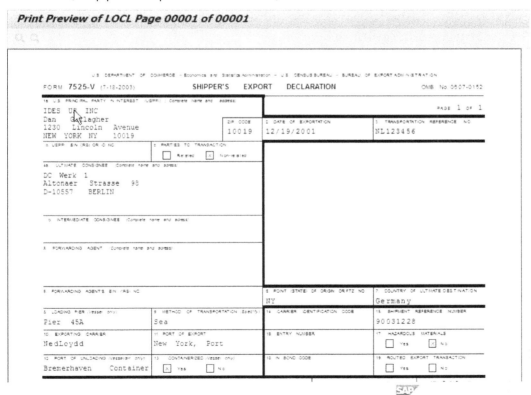

Bill.Doc.	Item	Out.	Med	Role	Name 1	City
90746558			1	RE	Customer Name	City
90746559			1	RE		
90746560			1	RE		
90746561			1	RE		
90746562			1	RE		
90746568			1	RE		
90746569			1	RE		
90746570			1	RE		
90746571			1	RE		
90746576			1	RE		
90746577			1	RE		
90746583			1	RE		
90746584			1	RE		
90746585			1	RE		

This is an example of an international invoice, also provided on SAP standard (shippers export declaration).

Functionality – Determining Printers for Invoices

Creating Output Determination for Invoices	
Menu Path	Sap Menu > Logistics > Sales and Distribution > Master Data > Output > Billing Document
Transaction	VV31

For the printers to be determined automatically on the invoices (as opposed to the users typing them every time), they need to have been defined.

This information is considered master data and not configuration, as the printers can change quite frequently.

This process follows the same logic as the pricing determination, where we need an output condition to determine the document type of the delivery to print (each one of the different formats will normally have a particular output condition).

❖ In this transaction, enter the output type for the delivery note and then select the enter icon.

Example: LD00 (Standard SAP delivery form).

You will get the screen to select the key combinations, so you need to select the appropriate option. In this example, you will enter the printer determination for the sales organization/billing type combination

Note: In this case, you will have the same printer for the whole sales organization and billing type. This printer will be the default printer by the user. This works if a particular user is generating the document, but will not be the best option if the documents are being generated on background.

If you are printing in background, it is recommended to determine a particular printer where the documents will be printed out from.

❖ Once you know the correct key combination, select the enter icon and the screen will enter the different condition records for the combination.

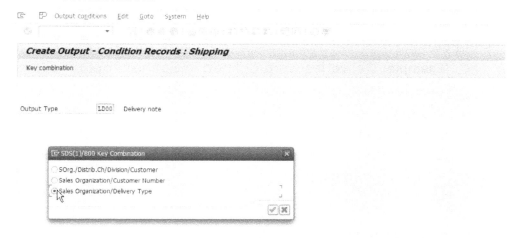

Depending on the condition type and its parameters, you will need to enter the correct information. This particular example uses sales organization/delivery type, as it is the most generic combination.

Note: If you need to have a different printer for a particular customer/ division, you can also create an additional record for that exception.

For each document type that will use the desired format, you need to enter an independent line (called condition record) indicating:

• Partner function to use as default.

• Print medium: Normally 1 (for printout), but can differ.

    o **Example**: 5 – Send by mail

• Time: This parameter is very important. It will determine the time when the delivery will be printed out.

    o 1 – With a job: Deliveries will not be printed out until a particular job is executed.

    o 2 – With a programmed time: Deliveries will be printed out at a set time.

- Example: Some companies run their delivery printout at midnight only.

  o 3 – With application own transaction: Deliveries will only be printed when the user manually executes the print transaction.

  o 4 – Immediately: Deliveries will be printed out as soon as they have all the conditions fulfilled to be printed out.

- Language

  o **Example**: Deliveries were defined in Spanish, but for some customers, they kept printing in English.

  o Normally, if you do not specify a language, SAP prints the documents in your customer's preferred language. Somebody had entered a condition for the customer in English (as an exception).

❖ To define the printer and other parameters, select the **Communication** button and enter the printer, number of messages, and the parameters on how the spool should behave (print immediately, release after output, etc.).

❖ After all the information has been entered, select the save icon for the changes to be stored in the database.

Functionality – Determining Printers for Delivery Documents

Creating Output Determination for Invoices	
Menu Path	SAP Menu > Logistics > Sales and Distribution > Master Data > Output > Shipping > Create
Transaction	VV21

In a similar way for invoices, in the case of the delivery documents, for the printers to be determined automatically (as opposed to the users typing them every time), they need to have been defined.

This information is considered master data and not configuration, as the printers can change quite frequently.

This process follows the same logic as the pricing determination, where you need an output condition to determine the document type to print (each one of the different formats will normally have a particular output condition).

❖ For this transaction, enter the output type for the invoice and select the enter icon.

Example: RD00 (Standard SAP invoice form).

❖ The screen to select the key combinations will appear. Select the appropriate option.

o For this example, enter the printer determination for the sales organization/billing type combination.

Note: In this case, you will have the same printer for the whole sales organization and billing type. This printer will be the default printer by the user, and this works if a particular user is generating the document, but will not be the best option if the documents are being generated on background. If you are printing in background, it is recommended to determine a particular printer where the documents will be printed out.

❖ Once you know the correct key combination, select the enter icon and the screen to enter the different condition records for the combination will appear.

Depending on the condition type and its parameters, you will need to enter the correct information. For this particular example, the sales organization/billing type was chosen. So, for each document type that will use the desired format, enter an independent line (called condition record) indicating:

- Partner function to use as default.
- Print medium: Normally 1 (for printout).
  o Example: 5 – Send by mail
- Time: This parameter is very important. It will determine the time when the invoice will be printed out.
  o 1 – With a job: Invoices will not be printed out until a particular job is executed.
  o 2 – With a programmed time: Invoices will be printed out at a set time.
    ▪ **Example**: Some companies run their invoice printout at midnight only.

- ○ 3 – With application own transaction: Invoices will only be printed when the user manually executes the print transaction.

- ○ 4 – Immediately: Invoices will be printed out as soon as they have all the conditions fulfilled to be printed out.

  - ▪ **Example**: If you set a condition that the invoice can be only printed after being posted to accounting, then once the document is saved and has been confirmed posted to accounting, the system will print the document.

  - ▪ **Note**: In a real life example, there was a condition like this where goods were ready to be shipped, but an accounting problem was preventing the invoices from going to FI. As a result, the invoices were not printed.

- Language

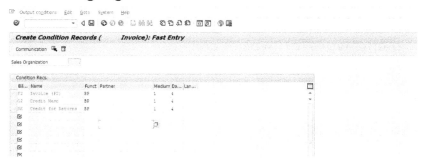

- ❖ After all the information is entered, select the save icon for the changes to be stored in the database.

10.2. CONFIGURATION

The functionality to determine an invoice or delivery note printed form follows the condition technique mentioned in previous chapters.

Here will be covered the most common functionality of creating a new output type for an invoice and including it in the output procedure determination.

Configuration – Creating a New Output Type for Invoices

The output types for invoices are the particular formats a company needs to accompany its invoicing needs.

Example: An invoice in the general form an invoice list, etc.

In Standard, SAP provides several output types that can cover the minimum requirements. It also provides a generic form that will need to be adapted for your company (at least the company logo will need to be replaced). This is done by ABAP.

The most common output types for invoices are:

- RD00 – Invoice
- LR00 – Invoice list

If you need to adapt the form (which you probably will), then the recommended procedure is to make a copy of the standard output type and output form:

Creating Output Determination for Delivery Documents	
Menu Path	SPRO > SD > Basic Functions > Output Control > Output Determination > Output Determination Using the Condition Technique > Maintain Output Types
Transaction	V/40

❖ First, copy your reference document:

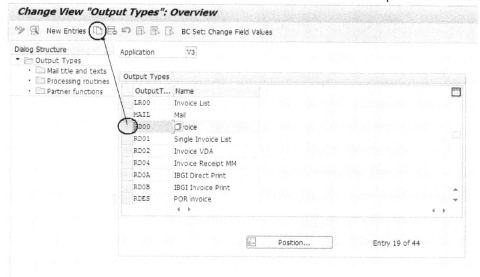

❖ Enter the new output ID, as well as its description and the additional parameters relevant for this configuration:

| General data | Default values | Time | Storage system | Print | Mail | Sort order |

Dispatch time	1 Send with periodically scheduled job ▼
Transmission Medium	1 Print output ▼
Partner Function	BP	Bill-to party
Communication strategy	

The main parameters to do this are:

Field	Use
Access Sequence	How the system will look for the conditions declared for the output type generated.
A c c e s s t o Conditions	If the system will look for conditions declared for the output or will take them from the customer master record. It is recommended that it be activated.
Multiple Issuing	If activated, you will be able to send the same document several times. For invoices, this is normally deactivated, as you will want to send the document only once to the customer. **Note**: if you need a "reprint" of the document you will be able to do so manually, but this is to avoid sending repeatedly on accident.
Change Output	Only used if you will send a change document to the customer.
Dispatch Time	When the document is going to be printed. 1 – Send by periodic job –Send it on a job that runs at a certain time. 2 – Send with job – With additional time –Send it on a job that runs at specific times. 3 – Send with application own transaction – For billing; means that the user manually has to go to transaction VF31, select the invoices they want to print and execute to print. 4 – Immediately – For billing means the invoice will be sent to printer (or via email) right away after being created.

Field	Use
Transmission Medium	Default is 1 (Printer); can be overridden by the condition records.
Partner Function	The information for this partner will be taken into the documentation to print. **Example**: BP – Payer –Information (name, address) will be printed on the invoice.
Communication Strategy	If using transmission medium other than printer (email, internet, etc.), you need to determine how the system will send the information.

The following section (mail title and texts) will define how the information will be displayed on the texts.

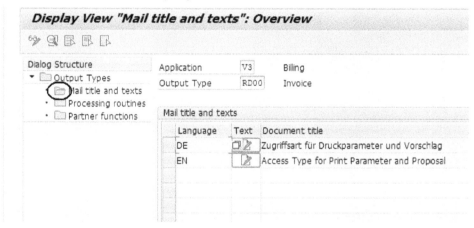

The processing routines contain all the logic and format to print the invoice. Any modifications to it need to be done by the ABAP team. n case they copy the standard form and create a new program/smart form, this will be the place where you change the name of the programs or forms.

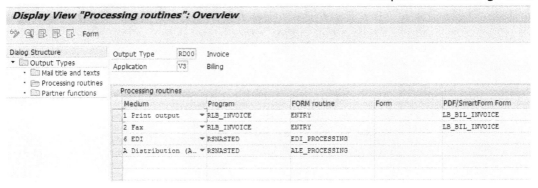

❖ For the partner functions, include the medium and the partner function to be used:

❖ After all the data has been entered, save the changes for them to be stored in the database.

Configuration – Maintain Output Determination Procedure

Menu Path	SPRO > SD > Basic Functions > Output Control > Output Determination > Output Determination Using the Condition Technique > Maintain Output Determination for Billing Documents > Maintain Output Determination Procedure
Transaction	SPRO

The output determination procedure will determine all the possible documents, which can be printed out for a particular document type invoice.

❖ Once output types have been defined, include them on the output determination procedure. To do this, double-click on the preferred procedure or select it and use the detail button:

Within the control data will be found the different output types, and these need to include your newly created output.

Note: The step where the output will be added is very important, as it will determine the timing when the output time will be found.

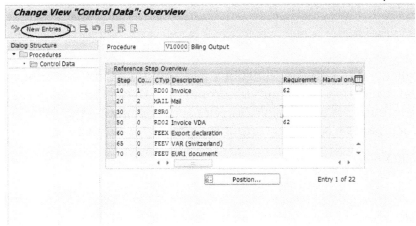

❖ Once the output type has been included, save the changes for them to be stored in the database.

Configuration – Output Procedure Determination

	Creating Output Determination for Delivery Documents		
Menu Path	SPRO > SD > Basic Functions > Output Control > Output Determination > Output Determination Using the Condition Technique > Maintain Output Determination for Billing Documents > Assign Output Determination Procedure		
Transaction	V/25		

Once you have your output procedure and the output type, you can assign the corresponding output to each of the document types.

Note: On this screen, you will be able to assign the procedures to an existing invoice type and add new lines in this screen.

If for some reason your invoice document type does not appear on the list, you need to go back to your invoice definition and review it.

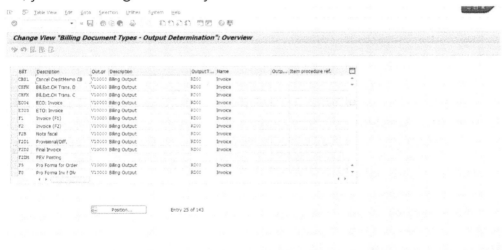

11. RETURNS

Uses and Functionality

In the sales process, it is not uncommon to have returns from customer or the need to cancel a document due to incorrect data (prices, quantities, etc.), so there needs to be a vehicle for canceling the transactions.

All returns, cancellations, and most corrections require a new set of documents to cancel/reverse the process.

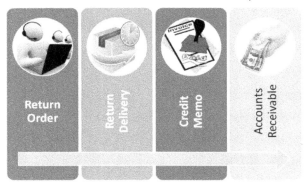

So, if a particular process was followed for a normal sales order, the returns process is similar.

As evidenced below, the returns process is similar to a normal sales order. However, different document types do apply.

Operation	Document Type – Sales	Document Type – Returns
Create a sales order (VA01)	OR – Standard order	RE – Returns
Create a delivery (VL01N)	DL – Standard delivery	LR – Returns delivery
Goods issue (or receipt)	Movement type: 601 This decreases inventory.	Movement type: 602 This increases inventory. Post returned inventory to special returns status

Billing	RE – Billing document	CR – Credit memo

Functionality – Commonly Used Transactions for Cancellations

This section will discuss the common transactions used for cancellations.

Note: These transactions are blocked in some companies due to security/auditing purposes, and the complete returns process mentioned must be followed.

Delivery Documents		
Transaction	Functionality	Comments
VL09	Cancel goods issue	This option can only be chosen if the delivery has not been invoiced. Otherwise, the invoice needs to be cancelled first. Executing this transaction will re-open the delivery document and allow changing quantities, batches, or even deleting the delivery document.
VF11	Cancel invoice	This option will cancel the original invoice by marking the original invoice as cancelled and creating a new document with the reverse posting. The original invoice is maintained in the system, just with a status of "Cancelled," and will still show on the document flow and reports. **Note**: This will re-open the delivery document and will allow further movements, like cancelling the goods issue.

The SD delivery transactions (like goods issues, returns, etc.) generate automatic MM material movements. These movements can only be reversed via SD transactions, as it is not possible to reverse them directly on MM.

12. REPORTS

Uses and Functionality

There are several standard reports that will allow you to get information from SAP. For ease of use, many of these reports can be downloaded to a spreadsheet.

Functionality – Common Reports List

The list of the most commonly used reports is included here:

Reports for Sales Orders		
Transaction	Functionality	Comments
VA05	List of sales orders	This option is the previous version with fewer search parameters. It has MASS update functionality for re-pricing, change plants, and change material or a new currency.
VA05N	List of sales orders	This is the newer version and has additional parameters for search.
VA06	Sales order monitor	
V.02	List of incomplete orders	Provides a list of incomplete sales orders (from the incompletion log).\n\n**Note**: If the order is complete (all required data has been entered), it will not appear on this report, even if it has not been shipped or billed.

VA14L	List of sales orders blocked for delivery	
V23	List of billing documents blocked for billing	
SDD1	List of duplicated sales order	Only considers sold to party/net value/ materials.

Reports for Delivery Documents		
Transaction	Functionality	Comments
VL06O	Outbound delivery monitor	This is a comprehensive report for deliveries. It can take you to the current list of deliveries already created (List outbound deliveries) or all the deliveries to be created or have a particular step pending (**Example**: List of all deliveries with a Pending Goods issue)
V_UC	List of incomplete delivery documents	Incomplete due to incompletion log.
V_SA	Deliveries collective processing log	

Reports for Billing Documents		
Transaction	Functionality	Comments
VF05N	List of billing documents	This option is the newer version with additional filter parameters.
VF05	List of billing documents (Older version)	

V.02	List of incomplete billing documents	Incomplete due to incompletion log.
VFX3	List of documents not passed to accounting	This report shows a list and allows for documents to be released to accounting.

Other Reports		
Transaction	Functionality	Comments
MMBE	Stock Overview	Detail stock report for one material.
MB52	Stock on Warehouse	Stock reports for the materials in the warehouse.
MB51	List of Material Documents	To display a list of inventory movements for a period of time.
MB5T	Stock in transit	Used with intercompany movements.
MD04	Stock Requirements	Helpful in determining if some items have not been confirmed.
MB5B	Stock for posting date	To determine the stock available at a particular date, considering goods issues and goods receipts.

The example shown here is for the list of sales orders. For every line on the selection parameters screen, there will be options to enter a range or individual values.

If you leave all the parameters blank, then the system will not apply any filter criteria and will bring all the information available, so the report may run for a long time (or even crash due a timeout). In this case, it is better to run the report in the background, where it can run for a longer period of time.

Functionality – Report Example

12.12.12.1.Selection Screen

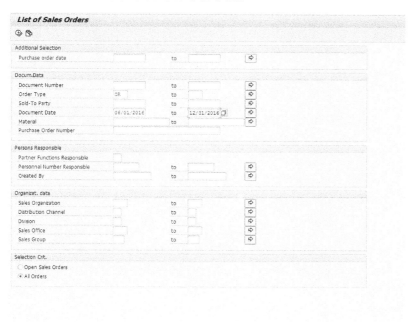

Button	Function	Button	Function
🗗	Variant selection	⇨	Additional ranges, exclude values, include ar individual value list tc filter
⊕	Execute (F8) The report will not be executed until this option is selected		

A report variant is a list of commonly used parameters that allows you to save the parameters to avoid typing them again the next time the report is executed.

12.12.12.2. Example: Execution Screen

Once the report has been executed, you can obtain the relevant information (according to the parameters entered).

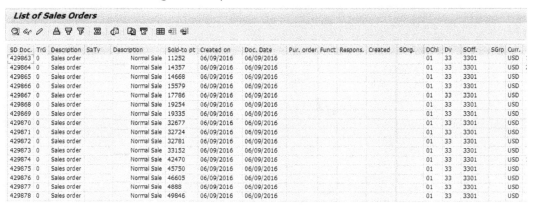

In some cases, the functionality to link to the document is available, either by double-clicking on the report or by selecting the line and choosing either to display or edit. You will then be able to see the original document.

Most of SAP will have similar functionality, so we are including here the most used buttons and its use:

Button	Function	Button	Function
	Show all the available columns for the selected line (on a pop up window)		Displays the selected document **Example**: On a sales order list, will take us to VA03 – Display Sales Order

	Modify the selected document **Example:** On a sales order list, will take us to VA02 – Update Sales Order		Order information on the report by the selected column (in ascending order)
	Order information on the report by the selected column (in descending order)		Filters information on the report according to the desired criteria **Note:** This is a filter that applies on the data shown in the report
	Summarize information on the report In some cases, sub-totals are allowed		Print preview
	Download a report to a file		Send report by email
	Update columns layout Allows you to hide, move, or show hidden columns		Select layout Allows you to select a previously-defined column layout
	Save layout Allows to save a newly created layout		

Downloading a Report to File

Given the common requirement of downloading a report to a file, this will be described further in detail in this section:

❖ First, select the icon for downloading a report to a file:

Next, you will get a window for the type of download required. The recommended options are:

• **Text with Tabs** (to be open in a spreadsheet)

• **In the clipboard** (for smaller amount of data)

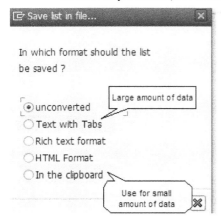

❖ After selecting the desired option, select the Generate button. This will provide us with a screen to indicate the path and file name.

❖ Select the 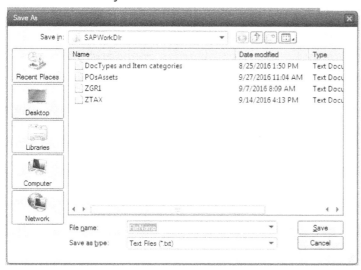 button to see the standard window to select the directory or choose a file name:

13. SUMMARY

Congratulations! You have covered the core functionality for the Sales and Distribution module.

After completion, you should be able to set up your organizational structure, create your basic master data, and generate the documents required for the order fulfillment process (sales order, delivery, invoice).

This module is integrated with many other areas (materials management, finance), and although there are many other topics still to learn, this will give you the foundation to build upon your skills and further your knowledge of the Sales and Distribution module.

Please note that the content covered here will be a starting point, and will probably not be enough to cover a certification test.

However, the topics you have learned here will help you to understand the material covered in the SAP Academy, and you can confidently strive for your training certification.

I wish you success on this new endeavor!

14. APPENDIX

14.1. SUPPORTED LANGUAGES

Language	ID
Afrikaans**	AF
Arabic**	AR
Bulgarian	BG
Catalan	CA
Chinese	ZH
Chinese traditional	ZF
Croatian	HR
Czech	CS
Danish	DA
Dutch	NL
English	EN
Estonian**	ET
Finnish	FI
French	FR
German	DE
Greek	EL
Hebrew**	HE
Hungarian	HU
Icelandic	IS
Indonesian**	ID

Italian	IT
Japanese	JA
Korean	KO
Latvian**	LV
Lithuanian**	LT
Malay**	MS
Norwegian	NO
Polish	PL
Portuguese	PT
Reserved- cuts†	Z1
Romanian	RO
Russian	RU
Serbian	SR
Serbo-Croatian	SH
Slovakian	SK
Slovene	SL
Spanish	ES
Swedish	SV
Thai	TH
Turkish	TR

** These languages are only partially supported.

14.2. COMMONLY USED TRANSACTIONS

This list includes a summary of the transactions discussed throughout the book, as well as some commonly used transactions not directly discussed, but that are worth visiting.

Transaction	Use	Comments
Sales		
VA01	Create sales order	
VA02	Change sales order	
VA03	Display sales order	
VA05	List of sales orders	
VA05N	List of sales orders	
VA06	Sales order monitor	
V.02	List of Incomplete orders	
VA14L	List of sales orders blocked for delivery	
V23	List of billing documents blocked for billing	
SDD1	List of duplicated sales order	

Transaction	Use	Comments
Delivery		
VL01N	Create delivery note	
VL02N	Change delivery note	
VL03N	Display delivery note	
VL09	Cancel goods issue	
VL06O	Outbound delivery monitor	
V_UC	List of incomplete delivery documents	
V_SA	Deliveries collective processing log	

Transaction	Use	Comments
Invoice		
VF01	Create invoice	
VF02	Change invoice	
VF03	Display invoice	
VF11	Cancel invoice	
VF05N	List of billing Document	
VF05	List of billing document (new version)	
V.02	List of Incomplete billing documents	
VFX3	List of documents not passed to accounting	
Accounts Receivable		
XD01	Create customer	
XD02	Change customer	
XD03	Display customer	
FB70	Enter financial invoice	
F-28	Enter incoming payments	
FB02	Change financial document	
FB03	Display financial document	
FB5LN	Display customer balances	
VKM1	Release sales documents blocked due to credit management	
Materials Management		
MMPV	Close period (and open the following period)	
MM60	Materials list	

MMBE	Stock overview	
MB52	Stock on warehouse	
MB51	List of material documents	
MB5T	Stock in transit	
MD04	Stock requirements	
MB5B	Stock for posting date	

Contacting the Author

If you wish to contact the author, you can do so at:

www.ConsultingDojo.com and suscribe to the Dojo Club to receive tips and news about future book releases and courses.

Follow us:

Twitter https://twitter.com/Consulting_Dojo

Facebook: https://www.facebook.com/ConsultingDojo/

NOTES

NOTES